God's
Answers
for
RealLife ™

30 *Biblical Truths that Will Transform Your Life*

Don Black

President, CornerStone Network

ISBN: 978-0-9859384-1-3
Published by CTVN Media, Wall PA

Printed in USA

CTVN
MEDIA

Table of Contents

CONTENTS

Table of Contents

FOREWORD

BY NORMA BIXLER

I applaud Don Black, our president of Cornerstone Network, for writing this book. In it, he encourages us to search out the scriptures so that we can live victorious lives as these truths get inside our spirit. *All scripture is inspired by God and is profitable for teaching, for reproof, for correction, for training in righteousness; that the man of God may be adequate, equipped for every work* (II Timothy 3:16-17).

Don shows us that through the Word we can overcome and have peace in the midst of any storm that we encounter. I know that you will be encouraged, educated, and moved to excellence as you let the Holy Spirit speak to you through the principles outlined in each chapter.

Prayerfully read this book and as you make God's Word the centerpiece of your life, watch for the wonderful way He will lead you! *Thy word is a lamp to my feet, And a light to my path* (Psalm 119:105).

WELCOME

I enjoy studying the Bible, to dig into its passages and discover how God has supernaturally made His Word the answer for every question in life. But it hasn't always been that way. For much of my Christian life, I relied mostly on what others said about God's truth. Pastors, Christian broadcasters, musicians, family and friends – these were my primary sources for answers. It isn't wrong to ask and learn from others; in fact, it is how the Body of Christ works. Each of us has gifts and callings that serve others in growing our mutual faith. But other people shouldn't have been the first place I looked to find answers to my many questions. God Himself wanted to teach me His truth.

> *The Holy Spirit desires to be our teacher. Jesus said of Him, But when He, the Spirit of truth, comes, He will guide you into all the truth; for He will not speak on His own initiative, but whatever He hears, He will speak; and He will disclose to you what is to come* (John 16:13).

My goal for writing and compiling *God's Answers for Real Life* is to help you better understand what the Bible teaches about specific life topics. Many of these have long been a part of the Cornerstone Prayer Partners' ministry materials that they would use on prayer calls. I have updated these subjects and added important new topics for your study.

That is exactly what I hope you will do with this book – study it. It is really a reference book. Place it beside your Bible and use it when you or someone you love has a question or faces a specific challenge.

My prayer for you is the same as the prayer the Apostle Paul offered for the young church at Colossae, a place he most likely had not yet visited before writing his letter. (The city was situated about 12 miles south east of Laodicea, and near the great road from Ephesus to the Euphrates. The site of the church is located near the modern town of Honaz in Turkey.)

> *For this reason also, since the day we heard of it, we have not ceased to pray for you and to ask that you may be filled with the knowledge of His will in all spiritual wisdom and understanding, 10 so that you will walk in a manner worthy of the Lord, to please Him in all respects, bearing fruit in every good work and increasing in the knowledge of God; 11 strengthened with all power, according to His glorious might, for the attaining of all steadfastness and patience; joyously giving thanks to the Father, who has qualified us to share in the inheritance of the saints in Light* (Colossians 1:9-12).

Don't miss what Paul asked God, that they would be... filled with the knowledge of God's will... so that they would walk worthy of the Lord... bearing fruit in every good work... growing in the knowledge of God... strong in His power... full of the fruit and gifts of the Holy Spirit... waiting with joy for the coming of Jesus!

Now that is a powerful prayer! In it, Paul describes the type of Christians who God will use to change their world. May it be so for you and for me.

I pray this book helps you reach this goal. The Holy Spirit is here to teach you right now. Reach out to Him in faith.

Come quickly Lord Jesus!

Donald Block

TOTAL HEALING

Sometimes healing can be seen as a controversial topic among believers, often relegated only to physical needs. However, our Heavenly Father is our Restorer. He can provide total healing for us in every aspect—spiritual, physical, and emotional—when we ask Him in prayer.

The Bible says:

Consider it all joy, my brethren, when you encounter various trials, knowing that the testing of your faith produces endurance. And let endurance have its perfect result, so that you may be perfect and complete, lacking in nothing (James 1:2-4).

Your afflictions are no surprise to God. He didn't create them but He will use them to shape your character. Take heart! God is able to get you through the struggles that challenge you today, through His mighty power to save, heal and deliver. In the New Testament alone there are 41 separate accounts of Jesus healing the physically or emotionally sick, and many of those gospel accounts are mere summaries of the healings of many people.

Know that the trial and affliction you are facing today is not a sign that you lack faith or are being punished for sin. It is a part of the Christian life for which Jesus prepared us when He said, These things I have spoken to you, so that in Me you may have peace. In the world you have tribulation, but take courage; I have overcome the world John 16:33).

God never promised that our lives would be trouble-free, but He has provided a way for us to rise above our circumstances. Sometimes that means learning to live in victory in the midst of the trial. The Apostle Paul discovered: *Because of the surpassing greatness of the revelations, for this reason, to keep me from exalting myself, there was given me a thorn in the flesh, a messenger of Satan to torment me—to keep me from exalting myself! Concerning this I implored the Lord three times that it might leave me. And He has said to me, "My grace is sufficient for you, for power is perfected in weakness." Most gladly, therefore, I will rather boast about my weaknesses, so that the power of Christ may dwell in me* (2 Corinthians 12:7-9).

While passing through the trial, remain steadfast in prayer. Let the love of God sustain you and the peace of Christ rule in your hearts (Colossians 3:15) through this time of difficulty in your life. Don't let fear of the unknown or feelings of hopelessness creep into your heart. Trust in the Lord's perfect timing and remember His promise to us in Deuteronomy 31:6: *Be strong and courageous, do not be afraid or tremble at them, for the Lord your God is the one who goes with you. He will not fail you or forsake you.*

Your Cornerstone Television family is lifting you up in prayer for a total healing in every area of your life that is broken or empty. The Lord has told us that when we – His children – agree together, He hears and answers our prayers!

MY PRAYER FOR YOU:
Heavenly Father, You know us inside and out; You designed our physical bodies to be fearfully and wonderfully made by the power in Your hands. Sickness, disease, wounds, and disability are nothing in Your sight, for You have dominion over all the elements of the physical and spiritual world. We are grateful for Your loving care for us, for the gift of salvation provided through the death of Your Son Jesus, and the gift of eternal life provided through His resurrection. You promised in Your Word that through the shed blood of Jesus, we could receive healing. We ask in faith, believing for that miraculous healing for Your child in the name of Jesus. Amen.

Stop Panic, Fear and Depression

Panic, fear and depression feed off of one another often leaving the person afflicted feeling hopeless, empty and exhausted. If you or someone you love is fighting these negative emotions, take heart! The Lord loves you and has perfect peace for your heart and mind in store for you. Nehemiah 8:10 reminds us, *Do not be grieved, for the joy of the Lord is your strength!*

Jesus' ministry to the oppressed and downtrodden has not ended! He delivers His children from emotional turmoil today. The Apostle Paul reminds the weary in spirit:

For I am convinced that neither death, nor life, nor angels, nor principalities, nor things present, nor things to come, nor powers, nor height, nor depth, nor any other created thing, will be able to separate us from the love of God, which is in Christ Jesus our Lord (Romans 8:38-39).

Sadly, some Christians believe that "true believers" never feel discouraged, afraid or depressed – as if Christians were meant to be somehow immune to these feelings. That's simply untrue! In fact, if you're suffering from depression or fear, you're in good company! When Job was stricken with disaster, he didn't speak for a week – and when he did finally say something, the Bible says, *Afterward Job opened his mouth and cursed the day of his birth* (Job 3:1).

The prophet Elijah also fell into depression: *But he himself went a day's journey into the wilderness, and came and sat down under a juniper tree; and he requested for himself that he might die, and said, 'It is enough; now, O Lord, take my life, for I am not better than my fathers'* (1 Kings 19:4).

King David, Jonah, even Jesus – all were sometimes bowed down and oppressed. The night before the crucifixion, Jesus told His disciples, *My soul is deeply grieved, to the point of death* (Matthew 26:38). If you are depressed or feeling oppressed, it doesn't mean you lack faith or have displeased God – it just means you are living in a fallen world. You can be touched by the Lord and restored to His joy.

If you are facing panic, fear or depression, know that there is deliverance available for you! Remember, your feelings are not always facts. I have learned to never trust my feelings. They always change. It is important to first try to identify the source of these feelings and combat the lie with the truth found in God's Word.

LIE: I have to live with these feelings of depression forever.

TRUTH: If you or a loved one is suffering from depression, there are several steps you can take to be proactive! If you have considered suicide or if a loved one has spoken of suicide, get Christian professional help! It is not true that those who talk about suicide are less likely to commit suicide — suicide threats must always be taken seriously. Sometimes, the cause of depression may be hormonal. If it has lasted for more than a few days, it's a good idea to go to the doctor and have a physical. If the cause of depression is a hidden physical imbalance, your doctor can address this and help you feel better. Otherwise, feelings of depression can stem from a multitude of different emotional or situational moments in your life. Talk with a trusted Christian friend, pastor or counselor about your feelings and try to pinpoint why they currently exist. Remember, the way you feel is temporary. God's help and blessing is coming!

LIE: I'm afraid that the pain from my past will always
hold me back.

TRUTH: The Lord knows your heart, and He understands if
you still feel hurt and hobbled by past pain. He wants to heal
and deliver you—whether you are experiencing guilt over past
sins that you committed or pain over past abuse by others. The
Lord wants to help you let go of the past; as the Apostle Paul
said:

> *Brethren, I do not regard myself as having laid hold of it yet; but one
> thing I do: forgetting what lies behind and reaching forward to what
> lies ahead, I press on toward the goal for the prize of the upward call
> of God in Christ Jesus* (Philippians 3:13-14).

When we feel grief over the sins of our past, we must humbly
repent and ask forgiveness of the Lord. Then we must believe that
God is faithful to His Word and has forgiven us. If we cling to guilt
and shame after God has forgiven us, then we are essentially
denying the truth of the Bible which says,

> *If we confess our sins, He is faithful and righteous to forgive us our
> sins and to cleanse us from all unrighteousness* (1 John 1:9).

God does forgive and cleanse our past!

LIE: I shouldn't tell God when I feel afraid or depressed,
because then He'll know I'm weak.

TRUTH: The Lord desires total intimacy with you—not just in
the mountaintops of your life but also in the valleys! Over and
over again in His Word, God gently reminds us that He will never
leave us nor forsake us (Hebrews 13:5, Deuteronomy 31:6,
Matthew 28:20, Joshua 1:5). He already knows what we are going
through but wants us to find new strength in Him. 1 Peter 5:7
reminds one to *cast all your anxiety on him, because He cares for you.*

Our Heavenly Father wants to help you—so friend, bring your burdens to His feet!

> *Come to Me, all who are weary and heavy-laden, and I will give you rest. Take my yoke upon you and learn from Me, for I am gentle and humble in heart, and you will find rest for your souls. For my yoke is easy and my burden is light* (Matthew 11: 28-30).

LIE: These feelings will never go away!

TRUTH: Fear, depression, and oppression may have a stronghold in your life at the moment, but they are merely seasons! Psalms 30:5 reminds us,

> *For His anger is but for a moment, His favor is for a lifetime; Weeping may last for the night, but a shout of joy comes in the morning. Glorious joy will be the result of this time of affliction! The Apostle Peter advises us: In this you greatly rejoice, even though now for a little while, if necessary, you have been distressed by various trials, so that the proof of your faith, being more precious than gold which is perishable, even though tested by fire, may be found to result in praise and glory and honor at the revelation of Jesus Christ; and though you have not seen Him, you love Him, and though you do not see Him now, but believe in Him, you greatly rejoice with joy inexpressible and full of glory, obtaining as the outcome of your faith the salvation of your souls* (1 Peter 1:6-9).

You can overcome panic, fear and depression to feel the joy of the Lord once again, especially if you remain committed to God and reliant on His power. Be secure in the knowledge that others are praying with you for your freedom. The Lord has declared:

> *When you pass through the waters, I will be with you; And through the rivers, they will not overflow you. When you walk through the fire, you will not be scorched, nor will the flame burn you* (Isaiah 43:2).

Isaiah 51:11 is God's promise that while you may feel discouraged today, there is a brighter morning ahead of you:

So the ransomed of the Lord will return and come with joyful shouting to Zion, and everlasting joy will be on their heads. They will obtain gladness and joy, and sorrow and sighing will flee away.

Know that your Cornerstone family has you in our prayers. We are lifting you up!

This prayer is for you to receive the power of the Holy Spirit to triumph over the hurts of the past, fears about the future, and discouragement for the present. The Bible tells us that when God's children agree together on something, He hears and answers our prayers!

MY PRAYER FOR YOU:
Heavenly Father, You promised in Your Word that through the shed blood of Jesus, we could receive healing. We ask in faith believing for that miraculous healing from feelings of depression and freedom from the oppression of fear. Your name brings power and redemption to our situations. We are thankful for Your faithfulness in our lives, Lord. We ask this in the Almighty Name of Jesus, Amen.

THE BATTLE FOR THE MIND

Our minds are the battlefield for the spirit, and our flesh is the vehicle that provides our spirit an earthly home. Don't miss this Kingdom Principle: We are a spirit who has a mind and lives in a body.

The abundant Christian life is achieved by renewing our minds with God's truth. Think about your brain as your spirit's computer hardware and the mind as your spirit's operating software. Our problem is not with the hardware; God's creation is flawless. The issue is with the software. We have allowed the world, the flesh and other factors to program our mind apart from the principles of God's truth. Renewing the mind is to remove the viruses and corruptions and replace them with God's Kingdom Principles.

Therefore I urge you, brethren, by the mercies of God, to present your bodies a living and holy sacrifice, acceptable to God, which is your spiritual service of worship. 2 And do not be conformed to this world, but be transformed by the renewing of your mind, so that you may prove what the will of God is, that which is good and acceptable and perfect (Romans 12: 1-2).

GOD IS YOUR SOURCE

Brother will betray brother to death, and a father his child; and children will rise up against parents and cause them to be put to death. You will be hated by all because of My name, but it is the one who has endured to the end who will be saved (Matthew 10:21-22).

In Romans 3:9-12, we read: *What then? Are we better than they? Not at all; for we have already charged that both Jews and Greeks are all under sin, as it is written, 'There is none righteous, not even one; there is none who understands, there is none who seeks for God; all have turned aside, together they have become useless; there is none who does good, there is not even one.'*

Only Jesus is sinless, and only when we trust completely in Him, do we find perfect peace. If a brother has interfered with your peace with God through his failure, let us pray with you for faith, love and grace to overcome that pain and be restored to your brother and to God.

Who is your source?
When the failure of others to do "the right thing" hurts you deeply, it's easy to become angry, bitter, disappointed or even depressed. When those we trust let us down, we can fall prey to despair. But if a loved one has hurt you, a friend or co-worker has betrayed you, a pastor or church leader let you down—however you have been hurt by another —you must remember: God is your source.

If you were looking to anyone else for your security and well-being, that was a big mistake. As Christians, we must place our faith in God alone, secure in the knowledge that He alone will never fail us.

Now when the people saw that Moses delayed to come down from the mountain, the people assembled about Aaron and said to him, *'Come, make us a god who will go before us; as for this Moses, the man who brought us up from the land of Egypt, we do not know what has become of him'* (Exodus 32:1).

Their attention had been fixed on the man who brought them up out of the land of Egypt, rather than on God, their Deliverer. Thus, when Moses failed to return from Sinai right away, the people turned away from God.

Don't allow anyone else's actions to turn you from God, your Deliverer. How often in daily life do we mistake the hand of God at work as the natural course of human events? We may thank our boss for a raise in salary and fail to thank the Lord for His provision. We may accept the congratulations of others on our new baby or grandbaby and fail to thank the Lord that the child was born healthy.

When we take the gratitude and confidence we should have for God and place it with other people, then we are not only guilty of idolatry, but we also run the risk of being disappointed by the faults of others. The Apostle Paul specifically said, *So then let no one boast in men* (1 Corinthians 3:21).

The people we choose to love and trust as close friends and family members should be worthy of trust. Our elected officials and church leaders likewise should be worthy of our confidence, but they must not be the objects of our faith.

God alone must be the one in whom we place our confidence. *In the fear of the LORD there is strong confidence, And his children will have refuge,* says Proverbs 14:26. Again in Proverbs 3:26 we read: *For the LORD will be your confidence and will keep your foot from being caught.*

If we keep our eyes on God instead of men, we cannot be hurt by their actions and failures. Yes, those dearest to us can wound us with their words and deeds, but we have the ultimate assurance that God will never hurt or abandon us.

At Cornerstone Television, we believe that if you have been wounded by the failure of others, God will deliver you from that pain and restore joy in your heart as we pray with you for His miraculous intervention in your life!

Jesus said, *These things I have spoken to you, so that in Me you may have peace. In the world you have tribulation, but take courage; I have overcome the world* (John 16:33).

The peace of the Lord is God's gift to you. As we pray together, there are some common sense steps which you can take to overcome the pain of rejection and experience a revival of the joy of the Lord in your life.

Realize that the pain you are feeling will pass as God comforts and heals you. *For His anger is but for a moment, His favor is for a lifetime; Weeping may last for the night, But a shout of joy comes in the morning* (Psalm 30:5).

- **Pray about it.** The Lord is your Father and your Provider. Tell Him about your hurts and your needs. *Cast your burden upon the LORD and He will sustain you; He will never allow the righteous to be shaken* (Psalm 55:22).

- **Worship the Lord!** The Bible reveals the one way to be sure that God is ever near: Psalms 22:3 (ESV) says *God is holy, enthroned on the praises of Israel.* Keep Him on the throne of your praise to Him.

- **Stay in the Word.** Hope and healing are right there in the Bible. Let its lessons help you. *Your word is a lamp to my feet and a light to my path* (Psalm 119:105).

- **Make a list.** List the people who failed you and why their actions hurt you. List the people who have your confidence today and think about how you would feel if they betrayed you. If you discover that your world is built on confidence in human beings rather than God above, take steps to bring your priorities back in tune with God!

- **Don't dwell on others' failures.** Yes, they hurt you, and you have grieved over it. Ask the Lord to forgive you if you have bitterness, and forgive those who hurt you. Then let the pain go and focus your attention on the things of God. The Apostle Paul advised: *Finally, brethren, whatever is true, whatever is honorable, whatever is right, whatever is pure, whatever is lovely, whatever is of good repute, if there is any excellence and if anything worthy of praise, dwell on these things* (Philippians 4:8).

You can overcome the pain that others have inflicted on you and feel the joy of the Lord once again, especially if you remain committed to God and reliant on His power, secure in the knowledge that Your Heavenly Father loves you.

Trust in the Lord for your deliverance!

God's promise when you've been disappointed...

Psalm 27:10-13 shows you that although men may fail you, God never will. King David wrote: *For my father and my mother have forsaken me, But the LORD will take me up. Teach me Your way, O LORD, And lead me in a level path Because of my foes. Do not deliver me over to the desire of my adversaries; For false witnesses have risen against me, And such as breathe out violence. I would have despaired unless I had believed that I would see the goodness of the LORD in the land of the living.*

Let the love of God sustain you, and remember that we are praying with you for healing from the pain and disappointment you have experienced.

PRAY WITH ME RIGHT NOW:
Heavenly Father, You promised in Your Word that through the shed blood of Jesus, I could receive healing. I forgive everyone who has hurt me. I release them from all guilt and ask that You lead them on the path they should follow. Also, I ask in faith believing for that miraculous healing for me from pain, bitterness, and disappointment. I pray these things in the Name of Jesus, Amen.

OVERCOMING THE PAST

Weeping may last for the night, but a shout of joy comes in the morning (Psalm 30:5).

Do you remember the story of the woman at the well in Samaria?

She was outcast even from her own people because of her sinful rebellion — shamefully drawing water in the middle of the day so she could come to the well alone rather than show her face when other women were there in the morning.

But when Jesus met her, He gave this outcast woman great news: *Whoever drinks of the water that I shall give him shall never thirst; but the water that I shall give him will become in him a well of water springing up to eternal life* (John 4:14).

Her past tragedies could be replaced by eternal triumph!

At Cornerstone Television, we believe that even as Jesus ministered to those who had been broken and hurt by the events of their lives when He physically walked the earth, so He still delivers His children from emotional turmoil today.

What are you to do with the past?

Sadly, some Christians insist that "true believers" do not have to deal with the scars of their past, as if only the knowledge of our Father's love makes every past wrong automatically right.

24

However, every day around the world, Christians and non-Christians alike find themselves hampered by the pain of the past, their future skewed because they have not properly dealt with the anger and bitterness generated by past events.

If you are struggling to overcome the pain of your past, it doesn't mean you lack faith or have displeased God. It means you are still hurting. And as such, the Lord wants to touch you and restore you to His joy.

How do you overcome past sin and pain?

The Old Testament gives us the example of King David, called a man after God's own heart. Yet, at the height of his strength and popularity, when he had become King of Israel and was much favored by God, David made a huge mistake! He had an affair with a married woman and then arranged for her husband to be killed so he could have her for himself.

Much sadness was to come from this. The child David and this woman conceived died, breaking David's heart. Although David sinned and betrayed the Lord who had raised him from nothing, God did not forsake David because he repented and sought forgiveness. He prayed:

Create in me a clean heart, O God, And renew a steadfast spirit within me. Do not cast me away from Your presence and do not take Your Holy Spirit from me. Restore to me the joy of Your salvation and sustain me with a willing spirit (Psalm 51:10-12).

When we, like David, feel grief over the sins of our past, we must humbly repent and change our actions or thoughts to be pleasing to Him. We must ask the Lord for forgiveness and believe that God is faithful to His Word and has forgiven us. We must then live in a way that is faithful to Him. If we cling to guilt and shame after God has forgiven us, then we are essentially denying the truth of the Bible which says, *If we confess our sins, He is faithful and righteous to forgive us our sins and to cleanse us from all unrighteousness* (1 John 1:9). God can and does forgive and cleanse!

But what about past abuse?

Rather than having guilt over your own sins or bad decisions, perhaps you are crippled by pain and lingering bitterness, or anger over actions someone else made which hurt you.

The peace of the Lord is God's gift to you. As we pray together, there are some common sense steps that you can take to overcome the pain of the past and experience a revival of the joy of the Lord in your life.

- If bitterness has taken root in your heart, ask the Lord to forgive you for this and all sins. One of our primary missions as Christians is to forgive others as Christ has forgiven us. Remember the story of Joseph from Genesis 37-50: His own brothers sold him into slavery, and from there he went to prison! Years later when Joseph had become a leader in Egypt, his brothers came begging food from him, and Joseph modeled forgiveness and compassion: *But Joseph said to them, 'Do not be afraid, for am I in God's place? As for you, you meant evil against me, but God meant it for good in order to bring about this present result, to preserve many people alive'* (Genesis 50:19-20).

- Pray about it. Psalm 55:22 says, *Cast your burden upon the LORD and He will sustain you; He will never allow the righteous to be shaken.* Instead of fuming or feeling hurt and humiliated, give your pain to the Lord.

- Worship The Lord! The Bible says *God is holy, enthroned on the praises of Israel* (Psalm 22:3 ESV). To keep the Lord ever near to comfort you, enthrone Him in your life through your praises.

- Immerse yourself in God's Word. Psalm 119:105 declares, *Your Word is a lamp to my feet and a light to my path.* It will guide you through the darkness of bitterness and grief.

- See the obstacles and pain of the past as part of a bigger plan. *And we know that God causes all things to work together for good to those who love God, to those who are called according to His purpose* (Romans 8:28).

You can overcome the pain others have inflicted and the guilt you may feel over your own sin, especially if you remain committed to God and reliant on His power, secure in the knowledge that others are praying with you. Trust in the Lord for your deliverance!

God's promise for overcoming the pain of the past:

First Corinthians 13:12 is God's promise that you can overcome the pain of your past and find perfect delight in God: *For now we see in a mirror dimly, but then face to face; now I know in part, but then I will know fully just as I also have been fully known.*

In the days to come, you will see the past as a tapestry God was weaving to your perfection, and you will understand how the Lord has been at work in your life.

MY PRAYER FOR YOU:
Heavenly Father, You promised in Your Word that through the shed blood of Jesus, we could receive healing. We ask in faith believing for that miraculous healing from the pain and bitterness of the past, in the Name of Jesus, Amen.

This prayer is for you to receive the power of the Holy Spirit to triumph over the hurts of the past. The Bible tells us that when God's children agree together on something, He hears and answers our prayers!

START FRESH, AGAIN!

Then they cried out to the LORD in their trouble; He saved them out of their distresses (Psalm 107:19).

Because of what the Lord has done for us, we need never live another minute in discouragement. No matter how bleak the circumstances around you may appear, if you are a child of God, your eternal fate has already been sealed – to live with God in heaven forever!

At Cornerstone Television, we believe that even as Jesus ministered to the sad and discouraged when He physically walked the earth, so He still delivers His children from emotional turmoil today.

The Apostle Paul reminds those who may be weary in spirit:
For I am convinced that neither death, nor life, nor angels, nor principalities, nor things present, nor things to come, nor powers, nor height, nor depth, nor any other created thing, will be able to separate us from the love of God, which is in Christ Jesus our Lord (Romans 8:38-39).

Remember, as you set out on your journey to revive enthusiasm and the joy of the Lord in your soul, nothing can take you from the loving embrace of your Father.

It's not a sin to be downhearted.

If you feel discouraged, does it mean you have lost your faith or that you are a disappointment to your God? Of course not!

A close look at the heroes of the Bible shows that many of God's people had bouts with discouragement when they felt like giving up…

In the Old Testament, Job was cited as a fine example of a godly man—yet he fell into depression and cursed the day he was born (Job 3:1). Moses, too, despaired over the faithlessness of the children of Israel.

King David, a man after God's own heart, also gave in to discouragement, and the mighty prophet Elijah felt so bad that he prayed for death (1 Kings 19:4).

After Jonah had led the city of Nineveh to repentance, he was despondent when God did not judge them as He had threatened to do (Jonah 4:1-3).

Even our Savior felt discouragement when He walked this earth. The night before the crucifixion, He told His disciples, *My soul is deeply grieved, to the point of death* (Matthew 26:38).

Feeling discouraged is just part of being human, and the Lord can help you to overcome!

What's the secret of staying enthusiastic about the Lord's work, happy in your job, and peaceful in your mind and family life?

One way to overcome discouragement is to recognize that God is with us—no matter what happens. When you are having a "mountaintop" experience, it is easy to feel that the Lord is close at hand; you see His blessing in your life, home, and business.

But when you are walking through the "valley" of life, you must remember that God is still with you. He is as real to you and loves you just as much in the valley as He loved you on the mountaintop. King David affirmed the Lord's nearness in his prayer:

> *Where can I go from Your Spirit? Or where can I flee from Your presence? If I ascend to heaven, You are there; If I make my bed in Sheol, behold, You are there. If I take the wings of the dawn, If I dwell in the remotest part of the sea, even there Your hand will lead me, And Your right hand will lay hold of me* (Psalm 139:7-10).

When you feel discouraged, remember that the Lord has not left you and will never, ever abandon you. He has promised: *I will never desert you nor will I ever forsake you* (Hebrews 13:5).

At Cornerstone Television, we believe God will deliver you from discouragement and restore joy in your heart as we pray with you for a miraculous intervention in your life!

Jesus said, *These things I have spoken to you, so that in Me you may have peace. In the world you have tribulation, but take courage; I have overcome the world* (John 16:33).

The peace of the Lord is God's gift to you. And as we pray together, there are some common sense steps that you can take to feel a revival of the joy of the Lord in your life.

Here is a perspective that may be a new one for you: You haven't been discouraged your whole life, and in the days ahead, you will feel joyful again. *For His anger is but for a moment, His favor is for a lifetime; Weeping may last for the night, But a shout of joy comes in the morning* (Psalm 30:5).

Take these steps to get out of the pit of despair:

1. Pray about it. When you feel discouraged, open your heart to the

Lord. *Cast your burden upon the LORD and He will sustain you; He will never allow the righteous to be shaken* (Psalm 55:22).

2. **Worship the Lord.** The Bible says God is *holy, enthroned on the praises of Israel* (Psalm 22:3 ESV). You can be sure that God is close at hand when you keep Him enthroned on your praises.

3. **Immerse yourself in God's Word.** All the hope in the world is found between the covers of your Bible. Let it encourage you! *Your word is a lamp to my feet and a light to my path* (Psalm 119:105).

4. **Count your blessings.** When discouragement closes in, make a list of everything in your life for which you are thankful. The Apostle Paul advised: *Finally, brethren, whatever is true, whatever is honorable, whatever is right, whatever is pure, whatever is lovely, whatever is of good repute, if there is any excellence and if anything worthy of praise, dwell on these things* (Philippians 4:8).

You can overcome discouragement and feel the joy of the Lord again, especially if you remain committed to God and reliant on His power, secure in the knowledge that others are praying with you for your deliverance. The Lord has declared: *When you pass through the waters, I will be with you: and through the rivers, they shall not overwhelm you; when you walk through fire you shall not be burned and the flame shall not consume you* (Isaiah 43:2).

Trust in the Lord for your deliverance!

Isaiah 51:11 is God's promise that while you may feel discouraged today, there is a brighter morning ahead of you: *So the ransomed of the LORD will return And come with joyful shouting to Zion, And everlasting joy will be on their heads. They will obtain gladness and joy, And sorrow and sighing will flee away.*

Let the love of God sustain you and focus on His goodness. King David wondered, *Why are you in despair, O my soul? And why are you disturbed within me? Hope in God, for I shall again praise Him, The help of my countenance and my God* (Psalm 43:5).

Friend, you will emerge from this season of despair. And remember that we are praying with you for the restoration of the joy of the Lord in your soul.

THIS IS MY PRAYER FOR YOU TODAY:
Heavenly Father, You promised in Your Word that through the shed blood of Jesus, we could receive healing. We ask in faith believing for that miraculous healing and deliverance from discouragement for Your child in the Name of Jesus, Amen.

This prayer is for you to receive a new excitement and zeal. The Lord has told us that when we, His children, agree together on something, He hears and answers our prayers!

OVERCOMING DEPRESSION

Do not be grieved, for the joy of the Lord is your strength (Nehemiah 8:10).

The Lord loves you and His desire for you is that you would be kept in perfect peace of heart and mind. Depression may afflict you, but the Holy Spirit is able to lift those dark clouds!

We believe that even as Jesus ministered to the oppressed and downtrodden when He physically walked the earth, so He still delivers His children from emotional turmoil today. The Apostle Paul reminds those who may be weary in spirit:
For I am convinced that neither death, nor life, nor angels, nor principalities, nor things present, nor things to come, nor powers, nor height, nor depth, nor any other created thing, will be able to separate us from the love of God, which is in Christ Jesus our Lord (Romans 8:38-39).

Remember, as you set out on your journey to overcome depression, nothing can take you from the loving embrace of your Heavenly Father.

Everyone has to deal with "the blues" sometimes.

At Cornerstone Television, we believe God will deliver you from depression as we pray with you for that miraculous intervention in your life! *Jesus said, 'These things I have spoken to you, so that in Me you may have peace. In the world you have tribulation, but take courage; I have overcome the world'* (John 16:33).

The peace of the Lord is God's gift to you. As we pray together, there are some common sense steps that you can take to defeat depression to:

1. **Realize that depression** is a temporary thing and don't focus on it as the central theme of life. *Weeping may last for the night, But a shout of joy comes in the morning* (Psalm 30:5).

2. **If depression lasts** more than a few days, get a physical exam. Make sure that you are eating properly and sleeping enough. Emotional well-being can be dependent on physical health, so take good care of your body. You belong to God!

3. **Pray about it.** Never doubt that God already knows what is in your heart and will not be shocked when you speak to Him in prayer. *Cast your burden upon the LORD and He will sustain you; He will never allow the righteous to be shaken* (Psalm 55:22).

4. **Keep busy.** Depression preys on idle time. When your hands and mind are full of the work at hand, there's little time to focus on depression. If work and family don't fill your time, give some of that spare time to volunteering where you're needed. It will help others and help you fight depression.

5. **Talk to somebody.** When King David was cast down over the loss of his best friend Jonathan and Jonathan's father Saul, he found release in talking about their lives and actions. *Saul and Jonathan, beloved and pleasant in their life, And in their death they were not parted; They were swifter than eagles, They were stronger than lions...How have the mighty fallen, And the weapons of war perished!* (2 Samuel 1:23, 27). Talking with a trusted Christian friend can be wonderful therapy when you are downhearted.

6. **Mind your mind.** When you find yourself dwelling on your depression and thinking self-pitying thoughts, train yourself to think of something else. The Apostle Paul advised: *Finally, brethren, whatever is true, whatever is honorable, whatever is right, whatever is pure, whatever is lovely, whatever is of good repute, if*

there is any excellence and if anything worthy of praise, dwell on these things (Philippians 4:8).

The Apostle Peter advised: *In this you greatly rejoice, even though now for a little while, if necessary, you have been distressed by various trials, so that the proof of your faith, being more precious than gold which is perishable, even though tested by fire, may be found to result in praise and glory and honor at the revelation of Jesus Christ; and though you have not seen Him, you love Him, and though you do not see Him now, but believe in Him, you greatly rejoice with joy inexpressible and full of glory, obtaining as the outcome of your faith the salvation of your souls.* (1 Peter 1:6-9).

Although today you may be very sad and blue, you will soon be blessed with glorious joy!

MY PRAYER FOR YOU:

Heavenly Father, You promised in Your Word that through the shed blood of Jesus, we could receive healing. We ask in faith believing for that miraculous healing and deliverance from depression for Your child in the Name of Jesus. Amen.

This prayer is for you to overcome depression. The Lord has told us that when we, His children, agree together on something, He hears and answers our prayers!

BREAKING SEXUAL STRONGHOLDS

GOD'S ANSWER

Finally, be strong in the Lord and in the strength of His might (Ephesians 6:10).

Right now, it may feel that your desires are so strong that you cannot even face them, let alone begin to overcome them. But the Bible tells us, *With people this is impossible, but with God all things are possible* (Matthew 19:26).

You can find faith to overcome the devil's attacks on your mind. Whether you struggle with ungodly desires, have an addiction to pornography, or are trying to end an immoral relationship, God desires to help you.

Second Peter 1:3 says of Jesus, *Seeing that His divine power has granted to us everything pertaining to life and godliness, through the true knowledge of Him who called us by His own glory and excellence.*

Christ has provided all that we need to live a godly life, including the strength to overcome temptations which Satan places in our path. As we pray together for your victory, we believe that God will show He is strong on your behalf. You cannot win this battle alone but with God all things are possible!

Bible's truth: Sex outside of marriage is simply sin.
The Apostle Paul admonished the Corinthian church: *Or do you not know that the unrighteous will not inherit the kingdom of God? Do not be deceived; neither fornicators, nor idolaters, nor adulterers, nor effeminate, nor homosexuals, nor thieves, nor the covetous, nor drunkards, nor revilers, nor swindlers, will inherit the kingdom of God*

(I Corinthians 6:9-10).

According to the Word, all sexual contact outside of marriage is harmful because marriage begins with the union of a man and a woman. Genesis 2:24 describes it this way: *For this reason a man shall leave his father and his mother, and be joined to his wife; and they shall become one flesh.* There is never a circumstance in which sexual acts outside of God's design can lead to anything good.

Some believe sex is just a natural act and not a spiritual decision. It is true that we are born with a sexual appetite; in fact, it is a beautiful gift from God. But when we allow our body's desire to dominate our spirit, it becomes sin. Then our decisions are not based on how God made us but on what makes us feel good.

The bottom line is this: Everyone is born with a predisposition to sin. According to Romans 3:23... *all have sinned and fallen short of the glory of God.* But that doesn't give us a license to sin.

You are not alone.
In some cases, when an individual comes to Christ, the Lord completely eradicates immoral desires in one clean sweep! But in far more lives, the struggle to overcome lust and sexual sin continues...but take heart – every Christian struggles to do good and live a holy life. And the Bible assures us: *No temptation has overtaken you but such as is common to man; and God is faithful, who will not allow you to be tempted beyond what you are able, but with the temptation will provide the way of escape also, so that you will be able to endure it* (I Corinthians 10:13).
We at Cornerstone Television believe that God can break the power of the destructive influence of sinful sexual acts as you trust in Him and commit to live a godly life. We are praying for that goal and have some suggestions to help you as you pray and seek God.

- Confess your sin, repent and ask God for His power to overcome.

- Stay out of areas where you know there will be temptation. If pornography tempts you, don't look for it on the Internet or linger near the magazine rack. If a lover tempts you, stay away from that person. If prostitutes are the problem, don't go where they are. Don't cruise. Don't go to a gay bar. Don't socialize with your gay friends in a setting where homosexual activity is possible.

- Pray about it. Never doubt that God already knows what is in your heart and will not be shocked when you speak it to Him in prayer. *Cast your burden on the Lord, and He will sustain you* (Psalm 55:22).

- When you feel weak, pray about it.

- Fellowship with God's people. Christian friendship will alleviate the loneliness which sometimes drives desire. It will fill the time to help keep you from lustful fantasy or action and will be a good, wholesome influence. Of course, never be alone with anyone who incites your lustful desire.

Confess your challenge to a trusted Christian friend, your pastor or a Christian counselor, and arrange for that person to pray for you and hold you accountable for your actions, according to James 5:16: *Therefore, confess your sins to one another, and pray for one another so that you may be healed. The effective prayer of a righteous man can accomplish much.* Don't let lust take hold in your thoughts; train yourself to think of something else. Study the Word. Meditate on God's goodness. Memorize Scripture. The Apostle Paul advised: *Finally, brethren, whatever is true, whatever is honorable, whatever is right, whatever is pure, whatever is lovely, whatever is of good repute, if there is any excellence and if anything worthy of praise, dwell on these things* (Philippians 4:8).

Although sexual desire is a strong drive and immorality a strong temptation, God in you can give you the power to overcome and live an abundant Christian life. Because you cannot fight this battle on your own, the key is your surrender to God. Let him rescue you.

Trust in the Lord for your freedom.
Practicing sexual immorality is clearly incompatible with
Christianity. Even if the act itself were not a sin, a lifestyle that
dishonors Kingdom Principles puts you on the throne of your
life and not Christ. *For through the Law I died to the Law, so that I
might live to God. I have been crucified with Christ; and it is no longer
I who live, but Christ lives in me; and the life which I now live in the
flesh I live by faith in the Son of God, who loved me and gave Himself
up for me* (Galatians 2:19-20).

The goal of every Christian must be total submersion in the person
of Jesus Christ, allowing Him to live through us.

If you have been living a lifestyle that worships your flesh, your
first step is to recognize that God loves you and wants to redeem
you. Repent of your sins (all sins!) and recognize that Jesus
Christ gave His life in order to spare you the punishment for
those sins and reunite you with God. Ask His forgiveness for
sin and purpose to sin no more. God will help you triumph!
And remember that we are praying for you! Call the
Cornerstone Television Prayer Line anytime.

FINDING FORGIVENESS TO START AGAIN

For as high as the heavens are above the earth, So great is His loving-kindness toward those who fear Him. As far as the east is from the west, So far has He removed our transgressions from us (Psalm 103:11-12).

God sent His Son Jesus to rescue you from sin because of His utmost love and compassion for you. Jesus demonstrated that love, according to Romans 5:8, by giving His life for us while we were yet sinners. Once we accept this amazing grace and salvation, *neither death nor life, neither angels nor principalities, neither the present nor things to come, nor any powers, nor height nor depth, nor any other created thing, will be able to separate us from the love of God which is in Christ Jesus our Lord,* as Romans 8:38-39 reminds us.

If you feel you have failed God and others in your life, take heart. Our God is the God of redemption and grace! He calls us to live a life of abundance, not despair over mistakes. As 1 John 1:9 reminds us, *If we confess our sins, He is faithful and righteous to forgive us our sins and to cleanse us from all unrighteousness.*

Many Christians believe that if they sin, they instantaneously are eliminated from eternal life. They imagine that salvation is as temporary as their next failure. By this skewed theory, Christians cannot sin, because the moment they do, they lose salvation!

This mentality is purely condemnation from the enemy. Romans 10:9 declares, *If you confess with your mouth Jesus as Lord, and* believe in your heart that God raised Him from the dead, you will be saved.

Nowhere in the Bible does it say that salvation is suspended if you sin. In fact, Jesus said: *My sheep hear My voice, and I know them, and they follow Me; and I give eternal life to them, and they will never perish; and no one will snatch them out of My hand* (John 10:27-28).

Nothing can take you from the loving embrace of Jesus – not even your sin or failure. But if you have failed, you must confess, repent, and seek forgiveness in order to restore a right relationship with God and allow His Spirit to work through you.

Sin happens as we live in a fallen and lost world. Even as the Apostle Paul confessed, *For what I am doing, I do not understand; for I am not practicing what I would like to do, but I am doing the very thing I hate* (Romans 7:15). Ultimately, God requires that you take responsibility for your own actions. James 1:14-15 makes it clear: *But each one is tempted when he is carried away and enticed by his own lust. Then when lust has conceived, it gives birth to sin; and when sin is accomplished, it brings forth death.*

In order to restore peace in your heart and overcome failures of the past, you must repent and accept the forgiveness of God. In this way, you will be *justified as a gift by His grace through the redemption which is in Christ Jesus* (Romans 3:24).

If you don't know exactly what to say in your prayer for forgiveness, you could start with King David's prayer from Psalm 51:1-4: *Be gracious to me, O God, according to Your lovingkindness; according to the greatness of Your compassion blot out my transgressions. Wash me thoroughly from my iniquity and cleanse me from my sin. For I know my transgressions, and my sin is ever before me. Against You, You only, I have sinned and done what is evil in Your sight, so that You are justified when You speak and blameless when You judge.*

Once you have repented, you must accept in faith that the Lord has forgiven you and move forward from the past! If you refuse to forgive yourself and continue dwelling on your failure, the sin becomes a form of idolatry; you are focusing more on your sin than on God Who has already forgiven you!

Accept the grace God has so willingly given to you and walk with God in holiness. When Jesus was confronted with a woman who had committed a moral failure, He forgave her sin and then commanded, *Go. From now on, sin no more* (John 8:11).

Isaiah 51:11 promises a brighter morning ahead of you: *So the ransomed of the Lord will return and come with joyful shouting to Zion, and everlasting joy will be on their heads. They will obtain gladness and joy, And sorrow and sighing will flee away.*

The Lord has told us that when His children agree together on something, He hears and answers our prayers!

MY PRAYER FOR YOU:
Heavenly Father, Your Son Jesus provided the free gift of salvation, and we thank You. Please make Your forgiveness real in the heart and life of Your child, and provide the power of Your Holy Spirit for a joyful, holy life. In Jesus' Name, Amen.

HOPE FOR THE HOPELESS

Then they cried out to the LORD in their trouble; He saved them out of their distresses (Psalm 107:19).

God can and does miraculously intervene in the lives of His children; so be strong in faith. Your miracle may be just around the corner!

We at Cornerstone Television believe that even as Jesus restored hope to the hopeless while he physically walked this earth, He still provides the power through His Holy Spirit to overcome our struggles today.

Consider it all joy, my brethren, when you encounter various trials, knowing that the testing of your faith produces endurance. And let endurance have its perfect result, so that you may be perfect and complete, lacking in nothing (James 1:2-4).

Your troubles are no surprise to God, and in fact, He may be using them to shape your character. Take heart! God is also able to deliver you out of the struggles which encompass you today through His mighty power to save, heal, and deliver.

Where's the sin?

In Jesus' day, religious people thought that struggles and trials in a believer's life signaled hidden sin—the suffering person must be out of God's will. But Jesus disagreed: *As He passed by, He saw a man blind from birth. And His disciples asked Him, 'Rabbi, who sinned, this man or his parents, that he would be born blind?' Jesus answered, 'It was neither that this man sinned, nor his parents; but it was so that the works of God might be displayed in him'* (John 9:1-3).

Jesus restored the man's sight to show the power of God! Today, some Christians still persist in believing that if we follow a certain sin-free formula derived from the Scriptures, then we will never be persecuted or afflicted, never be sick or in financial need. They look on their suffering Christian brothers and believe there must be some hidden sin in their lives.

But it's just not so. The trial and affliction you are facing today is not a sign that you lack faith or that it is a punishment for sin. It is a part of the Christian life for which Jesus prepared us when He said, *In the world you have tribulation, but take courage; I have overcome the world* (John 16:33).

The Lord takes pleasure in delivering us from our troubles through the demonstration of His power through the Holy Spirit.

God's intent was never that His children would be without struggle in their lives, but He did provide a way for us to rise above them. Sometimes that means learning to live in victory even in the midst of the trial. The Apostle Paul discovered: *Because of the surpassing greatness of the revelations, for this reason, to keep me from exalting myself, there was given me a thorn in the flesh, a messenger of Satan to torment me – to keep me from exalting myself! Concerning this I implored the Lord three times that it might leave me. And He has said to me, 'My grace is sufficient for you, for power is perfected in weakness.' Most gladly, therefore, I will rather boast about my weaknesses, so that the power of Christ may dwell in me* (2 Corinthians 12:7-9).

It may be that you, like Paul, must live with your trouble and learn to let the strength of Christ support you through this trial. But the Bible also clearly demonstrates that God can miraculously bulldoze the obstacles in our path to victory. God uses the struggles and problems of life to teach and instruct us about patience and faith in Him. It is our responsibility as

Christians to bear these trials bravely and wait for God's deliverance. At Cornerstone Television, we believe God will deliver you from your troubles as we pray with you for that miraculous intervention in your life!

The key to victory comes in the knowledge that no matter how insurmountable your struggles may seem, they are no match for the grace of God and the power of His Holy Spirit to deliver.

The Bible says, *And we know that God causes all things to work together for good to those who love God, to those who are called according to His purpose* (Romans 8:28).

If you believe that, then you must believe that the trouble facing you today is part of God's divine plan and eventually it will work in your favor. With that assurance from God, you can have faith that your prayers for deliverance will be answered, and that when you are triumphant, you will be closer to the perfection God has in mind for you.

In the meantime, you can have God's peace in your heart, in spite of the circumstances. There are some common sense steps that you can take to keep your trials from getting you down:

- **Get the big picture.** Focus on the fact that today's struggles are only temporary. You have hope for the future! *For His anger is but for a moment, His favor is for a lifetime; Weeping may last for the night, But a shout of joy comes in the morning* (Psalm 30:5).

- **Pray about it.** God wants you to bring your needs to Him in prayer. *Cast your burden upon the LORD and He will sustain you; He will never allow the righteous to be shaken* (Psalm 55:22).

- **Worship the Lord.** The Bible says *God is holy, enthroned on the praises of Israel* (Psalm 22:3 ESV). Keep Him on the throne of your praise to Him.

- **Study God's Word.** In the darkness of despair, *Your word is a lamp to my feet And a light to my path* (Psalm 119:105).

- **Count your blessings.** Make a list of everything in your life for which you are thankful, and it will help turn your thoughts from despair to beauty. The Apostle Paul advised: *Finally, brethren, whatever is true, whatever is honorable, whatever is right, whatever is pure, whatever is lovely, whatever is of good repute, if there is any excellence and if anything worthy of praise, dwell on these things* (Philippians 4:8).

You can overcome circumstances and feel the joy of the Lord. The Lord has declared: *When you pass through the waters, I will be with you; And through the rivers, they will not overflow you. When you walk through the fire, you will not be scorched, Nor will the flame burn you.* (Isaiah 43:2).

Trust in the Lord for your deliverance!

God's promise when you feel overwhelmed by trouble:
I will lift up my eyes to the mountains; From where shall my help come? My help comes from the LORD, Who made heaven and earth. He will not allow your foot to slip; He who keeps you will not slumber. Behold, He who keeps Israel will neither slumber nor sleep. The LORD is your keeper; The LORD is your shade on your right hand (Psalms 121:1-5).

Let the love of God sustain you and remember that we are praying with you for victory!

MY PRAYER FOR YOU:

Heavenly Father, You promised in Your Word that we could be more than conquerors. We ask in faith believing for that miraculous power to be released in the life of Your child, providing deliverance from struggles and trials. In the Name of Jesus we pray, Amen.

The Lord has told us that when we, His children, agree together on something, He hears and answers our prayers!

HEALING FOR YOUR BODY

Then they cried out to the LORD in their trouble; He saved them out of their distresses. He sent His word and healed them, And delivered them from their destructions (Psalm 107:19, 20).

From the earliest days of Cornerstone Television's ministry, we have believed in God's miraculous intervention in the everyday lives of Christians.

We have preached FAITH to move mountains!

And we believe that even as Jesus healed the sick while He physically walked this earth, He still heals His children from their infirmities today. During our Savior's walk on earth, He spent his three years of ministry life pursuing three specific outreaches: preaching, teaching, and healing.

When you read the Gospels, you see that one reason Jesus caused a stir wherever He went was that He performed miracles of healing. No matter what His enemies said about Him, they never tried to deny that He had miraculous powers.

There are 41 separate accounts of Jesus healing the physically or emotionally sick in the Gospels, and many of those accounts are mere summaries of the healings of many, many people.

Jesus demonstrated once and for all that God wants to heal His children from their infirmities!

Can I have faith and still be sick?

Jesus never implied that sickness or wounds were the result of sin in our lives or our lack of faith. In fact, in one instance when His disciples wanted to know why a man had been afflicted, Jesus gave quite a different answer. *As He passed by, He saw a man blind from birth. And His disciples asked Him, 'Rabbi, who sinned, this man or his parents, that he would be born blind?' Jesus answered, 'It was neither that this man sinned, nor his parents; but it was so that the works of God might be displayed in him'* (John 9:1-3).

Jesus restored the man's sight to show the power of God to heal! Having a sickness or infirmity in your physical body does not mean that you are hiding sin in your life! Jesus never unmasked sin when He was confronted with the sick and lame. Instead, He promised the forgiveness of sin and gave the gift of healing!

Healing is the Lord's pleasure for us and His demonstration of power.

Our ministry to the sick and dying world must follow the example of our Savior's ministry: We must believe for healing and preach forgiveness of sin through the blood of Jesus.

And when we are sick in our own bodies, we can know that the Lord cares and is willing to heal.

Some Christians believe that we must show such staunch faith that we cannot admit if we are sick, or seek the help of a doctor—as if admitting the truth or asking an expert for help somehow betrays our faith in God.

Of course, this is not true. Competent doctors are a blessing given to us by the Lord; it would be silly to ask God for a miracle cure when we could get the cure we need from a doctor. You might as well say you're trusting God to feed you but you refuse to go into a bakery and buy bread!

Jesus' disciple Luke was a physician and there is no place in scripture where God condemns the medical arts.

But when doctors reach the end of their knowledge, or costs make it impossible for us to get for our children, or ourselves, the needed treatment, we can know that God has the power to heal—and that He can and does heal!

And if the Lord does not respond to your prayer for healing with a miracle, does that mean you are doing something wrong, or that God has deserted you? Of course not.

The Apostle Paul had that very experience: Because of the surpassing greatness of the revelations, for this reason, to keep me from exalting myself, there was given me a thorn in the flesh, a messenger of Satan to torment me-- to keep me from exalting myself! Concerning this I implored the Lord three times that it might leave me. And He has said to me, 'My grace is sufficient for you, for power is perfected in weakness.' Most gladly, therefore, I will rather boast about my weaknesses, so that the power of Christ may dwell in me (2 Corinthians 12:7-9).

It may be that you, like Paul, must live with your infirmity and learn to let the strength of Christ support you through this trial. But there is also the possibility that your miraculous healing will come in a touch from God!

There are many wonderful testimony stories of Cornerstone Television viewers who have received MIRACLE touches of the Lord.

For instance, one viewer named Donna was always getting sick. Her blood pressure was high and uncontrollable. She was constantly lightheaded. Donna had a pituitary tumor and faced the possibility of a brain operation.

"The day I found out about the tumor," she explained, "I cried all day. Then I turned on Cornerstone Television..." At that instant, the host of the flagship program led her in the Sinner's Prayer. Donna got down on her knees and prayed with the host.

"My life has never been the same since!" she exclaimed.

Donna's medication made her uncomfortable and sick. But, she kept her eyes on Jesus. She developed a daily devotional time with the Lord.

Frequently, she called the Cornerstone Television prayer line. This helped to keep her faith strong.

When the doctors told her that she would never have children, Donna replied, "You're not God!"

When she had another MRI scan, the tumor had miraculously shrunk. No other treatment was needed! Not long after Donna's healing, the Lord gave her and her husband two wonderful children. "When the hand of God is on something," Donna confessed, "nothing is impossible!"

Indeed, all things are possible through our God, so don't give up on your healing. If you've called the Cornerstone Prayer Line or sent in your prayer request, we are praying with you and believing God for your complete healing!

Today I want to pray with you for the divine healing which is needed in your life or the life of your loved one.

MY PRAYER FOR YOU:

Heavenly Father, You know us inside and out; You designed our physical bodies to be fearfully and wonderfully made. Sickness, disease, wounds, and disability are nothing in Your sight, for You have dominion over all the elements of the physical and spiritual world. We are grateful for Your loving care for us, for the gift of salvation provided through the death of Your Son Jesus, and the gift of eternal life provided through His resurrection. You promised in Your Word that through the shed blood of Jesus, we could receive healing. We ask in faith, believing for that miraculous healing for Your child in the name of Jesus. Amen.

This prayer is for your healing or for the healing of your loved ones and family members. The Lord has told us that when we, His children, agree together on something, He hears and answers our prayers!

Receive His healing touch in your body today!

STANDING STRONG

Therefore, since we have so great a cloud of witnesses surrounding us, let us also lay aside every encumbrance and the sin which so easily entangles us, and let us run with endurance the race that is set before us, (Hebrews 12:1).

Temptation comes in many disguises but always bears the trademark of overpowering feelings of a loss of control. Your desires may seem impossible to overcome, but you don't have to fight your feelings alone! The Bible tells us in Matthew 19:26: *With people this is impossible, but with God all things are possible.*

You can put aside every area in your life that causes you to stumble in your faith. Whether you struggle with ungodly desires, pornography, or immoral and toxic relationships, God desires to lead you to triumph over temptation.

Standing strong against the flesh is against our human nature. Only through the Holy Spirit at work within us can we deny our "old selves." Jesus reminds us in Luke 9:23, *If anyone wishes to come after Me, he must deny himself, and take up his cross daily and follow Me.*

This act of surrender is not a one-time decision done out of guilt or shame, but a daily renewal and choice. We must choose every day to deny our sinful desires and follow Christ because we need constant restoration and communication with the Lord. He is our strength in times of trouble. We will fail every time we try to overcome in our own power. The Apostle Paul confessed, *For what I am doing, I do not understand; for I am not practicing what I*

53

would like to do, but I am doing the very thing I hate (Romans 7:15).

When we give in to temptation, the devil likes to flood our mind with feelings of condemnation. It's so easy to feel defeated and lost when we make wrong decisions and sin, because it was sin that separated us from God in the first place. However, nowhere in the Bible does it say our salvation is suspended if we sin. In fact, Jesus said: *My sheep hear My voice, and I know them, and they follow Me; and I give eternal life to them, and they will never perish; and no one will snatch them out of My hand* (John 10:27-28).

Nothing can take you from the loving embrace of Jesus—not even your sin. But if you have fallen into lust or immorality, you must confess, repent, and seek forgiveness in order to restore a right relationship with God and allow His Spirit to work through you.

Sex is one of God's good gifts to us, so what's the big deal? As followers of Christ, we are called to live "set apart" lives. 1 Peter 2:9 reminds us, *But you are a chosen race, a royal priesthood, a holy nation, a people for God's own possession, so that you may proclaim the excellencies of Him who has called you out of darkness into His marvelous light.*

Our Heavenly Father only desires the best for His children. A life of sexual immorality is a model of the worldly lifestyle we have been called to abandon: *For all that is in the world, the lust of the flesh and the lust of the eyes and the boastful pride of life, is not from the Father, but is from the world* (1 John 2:16). Lust and immorality destroy your chances of fulfillment and happiness in marriage by creating unreasonable expectations of intimacy, dangerous health consequences, and compromising the total emotional, physical, and spiritual bond with your spouse. Romans 12:2 reminds us: *And do not be conformed to this world, but be transformed by the renewing of your mind, so that you may prove what the will of God is, that which is good and acceptable and perfect.*

God can break the power of the destructive influence of lust and immorality as you trust in Him and commit to live a godly life. Confess your sin, repent and ask God for His Spirit's power to overcome lust.

- **Stay away from it.** Flee immorality. Every other sin that a man commits is outside the body, but the immoral man sins against his own body. *Or do you not know that your body is a temple of the Holy Spirit who is in you, whom you have from God, and that you are not your own? For you have been bought with a price: therefore glorify God in your body* (1 Corinthians 6:18-20).

- **Pray for help when you feel weak.** Never doubt that God already knows what is in your heart and will not be shocked when you speak it to Him in prayer. *Cast your burden on the Lord and He will sustain you; He will never allow the righteous to be shaken* (Psalm 55:22).

- **Confess your problem** to your spouse, a trusted Christian friend, your pastor or a Christian counselor, and arrange for that person to hold you accountable for your actions according to James 5:16: *Confess your sins to one another, and pray for one another, so that you may be healed. The effective prayer of a righteous man can accomplish much.*

- **Mind your mind.** Don't let lust take hold in your thoughts; train yourself to think of something else. Study the Word. Meditate on God's goodness. Memorize Scripture. The Apostle Paul advised: *Finally, brethren, whatever is true, whatever is honorable, whatever is right, whatever is pure, whatever is lovely, whatever is of good repute, if there is any excellence and if anything worthy of praise, dwell on these things* (Philippians 4:8).

God promises that although you may feel trapped and powerless in the grip of immoral desires, He will not let you fall: *No temptation has overtaken you but such as is common to man; and God is faithful, who will not allow you to be tempted beyond what you are able, but with the temptation will provide the way of escape also, so that you will be able to endure it* (1 Corinthians 10:13).

Remember that we are praying with you for your victory over temptation.

MY PRAYER FOR YOU:

Heavenly Father, We are grateful for the gifts of physical pleasure and imagination, and thankful for the sacred institution of marriage. We ask that You give your child the power needed to honor You in all areas of life, most especially strength to overcome ungodly desires and immorality. We make this request in Jesus' Name. Amen.

FORGIVENESS

For if you forgive others for their transgressions, your heavenly Father will also forgive you. But if you do not forgive others, then your Father will not forgive your transgressions (Matthew 6:14-15).

As followers of Christ, grace should be the basic building block of our lives. However, often believers find themselves struggling to forgive—not just others, but themselves. Pain from past hurt, rejection or sin turns quickly into bitterness and anger in the life of the person hurting. Christians are not immune to this pain, as if somehow following Christ removes you from life's battles. In fact, Jesus reminds us in John 16:33: *In the world you have tribulation, but take courage; I have overcome the world.* By overcoming the anger and bitterness in our hearts, we can move forward to freedom though forgiveness.

According to an old proverb, bitterness is like drinking poison and expecting the other person to get sick. We stay angry in order to justify the hurt inflicted upon us and try to subliminally punish the other person. However, this bitterness rarely has the desired effect on the other person, instead solely wounding the bitter party. As James 1:19-20 tells us, *Everyone must be quick to hear, slow to speak and slow to anger; for the anger of man does not achieve the righteousness of God.*

Often, bitterness grows inconspicuously. Like a weed in a garden, resentment grows bigger and stronger while we aren't looking, until finally it consumes our lives. Bitterness can also be incredibly selfish, as it turns us into the perpetual victim. Our attention turns inwardly and on the wrongs done to us; we lose sight of God and on loving our enemy when we are devoted only to revenge.

Forgiveness goes against our very nature, but we are called to forgive others in obedience to our Heavenly Father, as He has forgiven us. God will deal with any injustice dealt our way. We can pray for God to deal with the person who has wronged us, but the most we can do is forgive and leave our anger behind. Jesus' words to us in Luke 6:27-28 are clear:

But I say to you who hear, love your enemies, do good to those who hate you, bless those who curse you, pray for those who mistreat you.

Remember brothers and sisters, God has forgiven us for the most unpardonable sins of our lives—past, present, and future. We have hope for eternal life and a relationship with God because of His unyielding forgiveness. This amazing grace should be our ultimate motivator for forgiving those who wrong us, even if we must forgive them for the same act seventy times seven times, as Jesus tells his disciples in Matthew 18:22.

When we choose to harbor unforgiveness, we are sinning, as 1 John 4:20-21 reminds:

If someone says, 'I love God,' and hates his brother, he is a liar; for the one who does not love his brother whom he has seen, cannot love God whom he has not seen. And this commandment we have from Him, that the one who loves God should love his brother also.

If you're struggling to forgive someone or recognize the telltale symptoms of bitterness in your life, take a moment right now to surrender this burden to God. He knows that you are hurting and wants to take care of this situation for you. By giving this anger and bitterness to our Heavenly Father, you are allowing Him to work in your life and bring you to recovery: *He heals the brokenhearted and binds up their wounds* (Psalm 147: 3). God wants to see you living an abundant life unfettered by old grudges and hurts.

Pursue peace with all men, and the sanctification without which no one will see the Lord. See to it that no one comes short of the grace of God; that no root of bitterness springing up causes trouble, and by it many be defiled (Hebrews 12:14-15).

Sometimes our struggle with forgiveness is not with others, but with ourselves. Disappointment over past or present failures can be just as crippling to our hearts as bitterness or anger. We might think we do not deserve God's grace and forgiveness, let alone a second chance in life. However, if you have asked God to forgive your sins and have accepted His gift of salvation, you are forgiven—no matter what. The Lord reminds us in Isaiah 43:25 *that I, even I, am the one who wipes out your transgressions for My own sake, and I will not remember your sins.*

The issue is not with whether or not the Lord has forgiven you —when you choose to live in denial of this grace, the problem is with your thought patterns! You might have prayed and repented of your sins but have yet to believe and walk in the truth of what Jesus has done for you! This is not an accurate picture of your life as a follower of Christ! 2 Corinthians 5:17 reminds us, *Therefore, if anyone is in Christ, he is a new creation; the old things have passed away; behold, the new has come!*

Live in the victory that you are forgiven by the Creator of the Universe, the King of kings, the Lord of lords, the One who removed your sin as far as the east is from the west (Psalm 103:12). Every time you feel defeated with condemnation or guilt over past sin, declare the Truth from His Word into the situation. Memorize verses that will help you stay centered on your true identity in Christ. You are a new creation!

Know that you are being covered in prayer by your brothers and sisters in Christ here at Cornerstone Television. We believe that when two or more are gathered together in unity, true change occurs! Pray this as you seek forgiveness:

MY PRAYER FOR YOU:

Heavenly Father, thank You for forgiving me. By your grace, I am saved and able to have a relationship with You. Please help me to forgive those around me, as well as myself. I want to walk closer to You and I know that by surrendering these hurts to You, You will take care of me. I love You and trust You. I know that You are for me. In Jesus' Name, Amen.

YOU WERE CREATED FOR A PURPOSE

For You formed my inward parts;
You wove me in my mother's womb.
I will give thanks to You, for I am fearfully and wonderfully made;
Wonderful are Your works,
And my soul knows it very well.
My frame was not hidden from You,
When I was made in secret,
And skillfully wrought in the depths of the earth;
Your eyes have seen my unformed substance;
And in Your book were all written
The days that were ordained for me,
When as yet there was not one of them.
How precious also are Your thoughts to me, O God!
How vast is the sum of them!
If I should count them, they would outnumber the sand.
When I awake, I am still with You (Psalms 139:13-18).

Your life is not a happenstance or a mistake – no matter what the circumstances of your birth or the way you were raised may indicate. God knew you before anyone else. He wasn't just aware of your existence; He designed you in a very special way. No one is just like you. In God's view, there is no other person on earth today who can fill your shoes. What I am saying may not feel real to you at the moment, but friend, let me assure you that it is a fact. Most importantly, you have God's Word on it.

So if God made you on purpose for a special reason, you may be wondering what went wrong? You may be living in a way that you question both God's design and care. In fact, even though you have accepted Jesus as your Savior, you may feel that He is very far away from you today. If this is true, then as the sage once asked, "Who moved?"

Here is the trap that many of us fall into. We had a wonderful encounter with God, maybe at church or with a loved one, and asked Jesus to come into our heart. But once we were born again, we continued on in life on the same path we were on before being saved. Many of us were very young. As we grew up, we made decisions that led us away from our spiritual foundation. We chose the wrong friends, went to places that tore at our hearts, created bad habits that at first felt good, and continued to fill our minds and bodies with junk. Then we wondered what went wrong.

The answer is sin.

I simply define sin as turning our backs on God's will. The natural man wants to do life his way. In the 70's, the saying was, "If it feels good, do it." This form of existential philosophy dramatically impacted my generation of Baby Boomers. It gave the illusion that we were in the driver's seat of life making ourselves the god of our world. With this attitude it was easy to take the next step and begin to worship material possessions and our "feeling" pleasures. We became narcissistic self-worshippers. We created idols of everything and turned our back on God. Even today, this is not only true for individuals but also for the way we have allowed government leaders to act.

What happened to God's design for us that was in place before we were born?

The modern church has done a good job preaching salvation and making converts. The area where we have dropped the ball is working to fulfill Jesus' Great Commission stated in Matthew 28 & Mark 16.

Let me ask you two very important questions. #1. Are you a

Christian? If the answer is yes, hallelujah! You have taken the critical first step. Now, for question #2. Are you a follower of Jesus – His disciple?

In Matthew 16:24 it says: *Then Jesus said to His disciples, If anyone wishes to come after Me, he must deny himself, and take up his cross and follow Me.* Let's consider again what He said. Here is my version, "Many people like to be close to Me, but if you want to have a part in the Kingdom work that the Father sent Me to do, then embrace the object of the death of your self- will."

MY PRAYER FOR YOU:

Heavenly Father, I am starting to realize that You really did create me for a special reason. I want to change the way I think about myself. My past is filled with doubt and a poor self-image. Now I am learning that what You started in me You will finish. I love You and dedicate myself to following You all the days of my life. Fill me afresh, Holy Spirit. I ask this in the name of Jesus. Amen.

WHAT IS A CHRISTIAN?

...but if anyone suffers as a Christian, he is not to be ashamed, but is to glorify God in this name (I Peter 4:16).

According to a recent Pew Research study, 2.18 billion (32%) people in the world classify themselves as Christians.

Surprisingly, the word "Christian" appears only three times in the New Testament. There, its usage indicates that it was a term of disdain, placed upon Christ's followers by their critics. We find it, for example, in Acts 26:28 on the lips of King Agrippa, an unbeliever: *Agrippa replied to Paul, In a short time you will persuade me to become a Christian.*

It is also found in 1 Peter 4:16, ... *but if anyone suffers as a Christian, he is not to be ashamed, but is to glorify God in this name.*

Early believers in Christ suffered persecution because they were labeled "Christians." In fact, in 1 Peter, being a "Christian" seems almost synonymous with suffering. The third use of the term "Christian" appears in Acts 11:26, where we read that *...the disciples were first called Christians in Antioch.*

Here is my point: neither Jesus nor His disciples came up with the term "Christian" to create a name or to market materials for their movement. People outside of the Church, to describe the believer's actions and lifestyle, first used the word in Antioch. The people in Antioch watched how these Christ followers lived and then began calling them Christians. The Greek word for

Christian is *Christianos* which means follower of Christ, whose root word in Greek is *Christos* which means anointing. So the word Christian literally means followers of the anointing in the original language.

Imagine what our world would be like if there were indeed 2.18 billion Christians following the anointing of the Holy Spirit!

Unfortunately in today's world, the term Christian has come to mean more about where you live and what type of church you attend then your spiritual identity. In our culture it has become a social description and not a moral and spiritual code.

This isn't true of everyone. There are millions of "Christ followers" in the world today. For these believers, their life is different from the world. They are aliens to this world's culture and look forward to the return of Jesus, the Christ.

Who can become a Christian?

The Bible is clear. God's desire is for everyone to be in personal relationship with Him through His Son, Jesus. *The Lord is not slow about His promise, as some count slowness, but is patient toward you, not wishing for any to perish but for all to come to repentance* (2 Peter 3:9).

Our Heavenly Father made the steps to salvation very simple. *...that if you confess with your mouth Jesus as Lord, and believe in your heart that God raised Him from the dead, you will be saved; for with the heart a person believes, resulting in righteousness, and with the mouth he confesses, resulting in salvation* (Romans 10: 9-10).

That is all there is to it!
1. **Believe**
2. **Confess**

3. **Repent**
4. **Ask**
5. **Receive**
6. **Rejoice!**

I asked Jesus into my heart at the age of eight while watching Billy Graham on television. Here is an exact copy of that simple prayer.

Dear Lord Jesus, I know that I am a sinner, and I ask for Your forgiveness. I believe You died for my sins and rose from the dead. I turn from my sins and invite You to come into my heart and life. I want to trust and follow You as my Lord and Savior. In Jesus' Name, Amen.

Friend, what if today you would stand before God in heaven and He asked why you should be allowed to come in – and you were not sure of the answer? I encourage you to do as I did and use this prayer as a guide to give your life to Him right now. Next, I want you to call or email us at Cornerstone and let us know You that you prayed that prayer. We want to talk to you and send you some free information to help you get started on the path to eternal life.

THE BAPTISM OF
THE HOLY SPIRIT

John answered and said to them all, 'As for me, I baptize you with water; but One is coming who is mightier than I, and I am not fit to untie the thong of His sandals; He will baptize you with the Holy Spirit and fire' (Luke 3:16).

The Bible teaches us that God is on His throne in Heaven and Jesus is at His right hand. So where is the Holy Spirit? Before we go any farther in this study of the baptism, let's talk about who the Holy Spirit is.

He is the third member of the Trinity (God the Father, Son, and Holy Spirit). I use the word "He" to describe the Holy Spirit. He is not an "it" or some mysterious feeling or random experience. He is God.

When we invite Jesus to come into our heart and save us, what actually happens in the spiritual dimension is the Holy Spirit enters us and transforms our human body into His holy temple. Right now Jesus in His Kingdom body is at the right hand of the Father in Heaven. The Bible tells us that He is there making intercession for you and me to the Father.

Not long ago, Benny Hinn gave me a wonderful description of the Holy Spirit; he said that the Spirit is Jesus without limitations. I asked Pastor Benny what possible limitations did Jesus have while He was on earth? The answer is simple. He was limited by the flesh. He could only be in one place at a time. But the Holy Spirit is everywhere at once. When we are saved, what actually becomes born-again is our spirit. At that moment our spirit connects to the Holy Spirit and we become a new creature. In fact, it was the Holy Spirit that convicted you of sin and provided you with the faith to call out to God to repent and ask for forgiveness. He is our constant companion Who leads us into all truth. He, the Father, and Jesus are one. Without the Holy Spirit, we would have no power to live a victorious Christian life.

What is the baptism of the Holy Spirit?

John the Baptist prophesied: *As for me, I baptize you with water; but One is coming who is mightier than I, and I am not fit to untie the thong of His sandals; He will baptize you with the Holy Spirit and fire* (Luke 3:16).

Jesus told His followers to go back to the Upper Room and wait. *Gathering them together, He commanded them not to leave Jerusalem, but to wait for what the Father had promised, 'Which,' He said, 'you heard of from Me; for John baptized with water, but you will be baptized with the Holy Spirit not many days from now'* (Acts 1:4-5).

Then 9 a.m. on the day of Pentecost, somewhere near 31 AD, this promise was fulfilled. *When the day of Pentecost had come, they were all together in one place. And suddenly there came from heaven a noise like a violent rushing wind, and it filled the whole house where they were sitting. And there appeared to them tongues as of fire distributing themselves, and they rested on each one of them. And they were all filled with the Holy Spirit and began to speak with other tongues, as the Spirit was giving them utterance* (Acts 2:1).

On that day God delivered the Church Age to this world. When the Holy Spirit fell on the believers, they were transformed from individual followers of Jesus into Spirit- powered members of His Church, the Body of Christ. The birth of the Church marked the beginning of the end.

'AND IT SHALL BE IN THE LAST DAYS,' God says, 'THAT I WILL POUR FORTH OF MY SPIRIT ON ALL

MANKIND; AND YOUR SONS AND YOUR DAUGHTERS
SHALL PROPHESY, AND YOUR YOUNG MEN SHALL SEE
VISIONS, AND YOUR OLD MEN SHALL DREAM DREAMS;
[18] EVEN ON MY BONDSLAVES, BOTH MEN AND WOMEN,
I WILL IN THOSE DAYS POUR FORTH OF MY SPIRIT
AND THEY SHALL PROPHESY.
[19] 'AND I WILL GRANT WONDERS IN THE SKY ABOVE
AND SIGNS ON THE EARTH BELOW,
BLOOD, AND FIRE, AND VAPOR OF SMOKE.
20 'THE SUN WILL BE TURNED INTO DARKNESS
AND THE MOON INTO BLOOD,
BEFORE THE GREAT AND GLORIOUS DAY OF THE LORD
SHALL COME.
[21] 'AND IT SHALL BE THAT EVERYONE WHO CALLS ON
THE NAME OF THE LORD WILL BE SAVED' (Acts 2: 17-21).

The world would never be the same, and now we are in the
final days of the end of this age.

The Greek word used for baptism is "baptizo" which means to
be immersed into something else. Jesus is the One who covers
us with His Holy Spirit. If you are a believer and have not
received this same baptism in the Holy Spirit, nothing stands in
your way.

Here are important facts to remember about the baptism of the
Holy Spirit.

• You have to be a Christian to receive the baptism.

• You need to have clean hands and a pure heart before the
  Lord. Confess and turn away from any sin for which the
  Spirit is convicting you.

• You must ask Jesus to baptize you.

• Receive His filling by faith.

• Worship God with all your heart. Thank Him!

The Dialect of Angels

In the Bible when believers were baptized in the Holy Spirit, they received a special language with which to pray. This is the language of Heaven, the dialect of angels. With this gift of a special prayer tongue, we are able to communicate with God in a very powerful way.

But if we hope for what we do not see, with perseverance we wait eagerly for it. In the same way the Spirit also helps our weakness; for we do not know how to pray as we should, but the Spirit Himself intercedes for us with groanings too deep for words; and He who searches the hearts knows what the mind of the Spirit is, because He intercedes for the saints according to the will of God. And we know that God causes all things to work together for good to those who love God, to those who are called according to His purpose (Romans 8:25-28).

Do you need help for your weakness? When we pray in the Spirit, He intercedes for us in the Heavenly language. This is a very important benefit of the Holy Spirit living inside of us. This supernatural gift of communication bypasses our mind's ability to understand and releases the Spirit to pray through us according to God's will! Why would anyone not desire this wonderful connection with God? It is in context to praying in the Spirit that Paul promised that all things work together for good. Why? Because he knew that when we pray according to God's will, that request will be answered.

Every Christian should seek the baptism of the Holy Spirit. Without walking in the Spirit it is impossible to be the witness to your world that God designed for you to be.

**Use this prayer as a model to ask for
the baptism of the Spirit:**

Jesus, I love You and want to have everything that You created for me. The Bible says You are the one Who will baptize me in the Holy Spirit. Please show me right now anything that I am doing that stands in the way of our relationship. I repent and turn from it. I wash my hands from that sin. I ask for You to fill me with the Spirit. You said to ask and believe, so I receive the baptism of the Holy Spirit now by faith. I love You, Lord, and thank You for giving me everything I need to live for You. I pray in the name of Jesus. Amen!

WHY GOD STILL
DOES MIRACLES

Remember those who led you, who spoke the word of God to you; and considering the result of their conduct, imitate their faith. Jesus Christ is the same yesterday and today and forever (Hebrews 13:7-8).

There are sincere Christians who believe that God does not work in the lives of people the way that He did in the Bible days. Some have been taught that the age of miracles ended with the death of the Apostle John, as he was the last disciple to die. Others believe that miracles ended when the Bible was written and printed.

My purpose here is not to confront these theories but rather to tell you why I know that God still performs miracles in the lives of His children. I believe because I have received. It is as simple as that.

If Jesus Christ is the same yesterday, today and forever, how can we not believe?

Jesus said something very interesting in light of this discussion:
Truly, truly, I say to you, he who believes in Me, the works that I do, he will do also; and greater works than these he will do; because I go to the Father. Whatever you ask in My name, that will I do, so that the Father may be glorified in the Son. If you ask Me anything in My name, I will do it (John 14:12-14).

What He was prophesying was that believers would do the

works that He did. Remember that in Jesus' ministry the blind were healed, demons were cast out, even the dead were raised. So why would He say that we would do even greater works if He knew that the age of miracles would soon end?

Friend, don't let anyone convince you that Jesus doesn't work wonders today. He does them to bring glory to God.

WHY SPIRITUAL GIFTS?

But you will receive power when the Holy Spirit has come upon you; and you shall be My witnesses both in Jerusalem, and in all Judea and Samaria, and even to the remotest part of the earth Acts 1:8.

The primary purpose for the gifts of the Spirit is to give the members of the Church power to demonstrate to the world the love and power of Jesus Christ.

> *...for the equipping of the saints for the work of service, to the building up of the body of Christ; until we all attain to the unity of the faith, and of the knowledge of the Son of God, to a mature man, to the measure of the stature which belongs to the fullness of Christ. As a result, we are no longer to be children, tossed here and there by waves and carried about by every wind of doctrine, by the trickery of men, by craftiness in deceitful scheming; but speaking the truth in love, we are to grow up in all aspects into Him who is the head, even Christ, from whom the whole body, being fitted and held together by what every joint supplies, according to the proper working of each individual part, causes the growth of the body for the building up of itself in love* (Ephesians 4: 12-16).

So also you, since you are zealous of spiritual gifts, seek to abound for the edification of the church (I Corinthians 14:12). Therefore our goal should be to establish, build, and encourage the Church with the spiritual gifts that the Holy Spirit has entrusted to us.

Revelation 4:11 says, *Worthy are you, our Lord and our God, to receive glory and honor and power; for You created all things, and because of Your will they existed, and were created.* After receiving

Jesus as our Savior, we are left to stay here on earth to glorify God and be living witnesses of His love, grace, and power. God desires to have a relationship with us through His Son Jesus. But He also wants to have a loving relationship with everyone else! That is why we, by His Spirit, need to do our part to help get His work done.

In John 15:8 Jesus says, *My Father is glorified by this, that you bear much fruit, and so prove to be My disciples.* By bearing much fruit, we glorify God, and we can only do this by abiding in Him and using our gifts to serve Him.

Are You a Missing Body Part?

You are needed in the Body of Christ. If you are a Christian and are not connected to the Body in some way, the Church as a whole suffers from your absence. It's like missing a part of your own body. You could probably live a normal life with just nine out of ten fingers. But your hands still wouldn't be able to do everything as well as if you had all your fingers. The truth is, the Body of Christ has missing parts. They may even be attached but are missing in action. The Church is called the "Body of Christ" for a reason. We are connected by our faith in Jesus Christ and sealed by the Holy Spirit into His Body.

A Unified Church

Being members of His body, we need to work together. I Corinthians 12:12 teaches, *For even as the body is one and yet has many members, and all the members of the body, though they are many, are one body, so also is Christ.* And in verse 14, *For the body is not one member, but many.*

Each of us is a specific body part. It sounds strange but it is a great analogy. In verse 27, Paul affirms, *Now you are Christ's body, and individually members of it.* When you read verses 13-27 you will see that Paul is telling of the importance of each member. He is also declaring that we need each member to function properly as a whole body. He says in verse 26, *And if one member suffers, all the members suffer with it; if one member is honored, all the members rejoice with it.*

We glorify God by getting involved.
In Ephesians 2:10, *For we are His workmanship, created in Christ Jesus for good works, which God prepared beforehand so that we would walk in them.* God already has plans for you in His Body. He expects you to use the gifts he has given you.

Growth Steps:
1. **The first step is to pray and have a willing heart.** Pray for God's guidance and ask Him to use you for His purpose. Ask Him to open your eyes and ears to His call on your life. He will point out a direction or calling upon your heart.

2. **Discover and develop the gifts He has provided.** He has and will provide everything you will need to accomplish each goal He has for your life. Our gifts are to be developed as we mature in the faith. Philippians 1:6 says, *For I am confident of this very thing, that He who began a good work in you will perfect it until the day of Christ Jesus.* Don't be afraid of what He will do with you. Step out in faith and let Him use you. The rewards will be great.

3. **Find your place in His Body.** If you are not sure what specific area you are led to serve in, but you know what gifts you have, match up with other people who share your desire and heart for ministry. God will use your service to strengthen your gifts and will work out the details in His time.

4. **Seek, knock and serve.** Faithfully serve in the small things and allow God to work in and through your life at His pace. Confidently apply your gifts whenever needed and humbly desire for Him to use you.

5. **Be a good manager.** God promises that if you are faithful

with a few things He will make you a steward over many things. I Peter 4:10 teaches, *As each one has received a special gift, employ it in serving one another as good stewards of the manifold grace of God.* Use your gifts at every opportunity to show the love, grace and power of God to others. This will produce fruit that remains and will glorify Him.

6. **Most of all, LOVE.** Use your gifts with love, for the glory of God and the building up of His church. I Corinthians 13:13 says, *But now faith, hope, love, abide these three; but the greatest of these is love.* Put on love in every situation, and every time you serve, make God the focus. My daughter recently said something to me that has really made me think. We were talking about truth and she said, "All truth spoken outside of love is brutality." She is so right.

MY PRAYER FOR YOU:

Lord Jesus, teach us to seek after all You have created for us but help us to only do it motivated by Your love. This I ask in the name of Jesus. Amen.

THE GIFTS OF
THE HOLY SPIRIT

But to each one of us grace was given according to the measure of Christ's gift. Therefore it says,
"WHEN HE ASCENDED ON HIGH,
HE LED CAPTIVE A HOST OF CAPTIVES,
AND HE GAVE GIFTS TO MEN" (Ephesians 4:7-8).

Have you ever questioned the purpose of the gifts of the Spirit? How many are there? Why did God include them in His design for us? He could have had the angels do everything without placing His Spirit in us. But that is not what He desires. The will of the Father is to bring us into an intimate relationship with Himself.

Is the Holy Spirit an important part of your everyday life?

He should be. The Holy Spirit brings to us the supernatural ability to be like Jesus. He is the conduit of God who equips Christians to live the abundant life Jesus promised. The fruit of the Spirit (Galatians 5:22-23) describe the temperament of our Heavenly Father.

The gifts of the Spirit reveal the ways of God to the world through the Church.

Through study of the scripture, I have identified 21 gifts the Holy Spirit gives to us. Most likely there are others that I have not yet discovered; God's Word always teaches me something new. The following overview will help you better understand just how much God loves us and what He has given us to put into our daily lives.

I have organized these Gifts into three groups to study.

Group #1 - The corporate plan of God
Group #2 - His power
Group #3 - His nature and His ways

Group #1 – Leadership gifts that REVEAL and DIRECT the CORPORATE PLAN of God

And He gave some as apostles, and some as prophets, and some as evangelists, and some as pastors and teachers, for the equipping of the saints for the work of service, to the building up of the body of Christ; until we all attain to the unity of the faith, and of the knowledge of the Son of God, to a mature man, to the measure of the stature which belongs to the fullness of Christ. As a result, we are no longer to be children, tossed here and there by waves and carried about by every wind of doctrine, by the trickery of men, by craftiness in deceitful scheming; but speaking the truth in love, we are to grow up in all aspects into Him who is the head, even Christ, from whom the whole body, being fitted and held together by what every joint supplies, according to the proper working of each individual part, causes the growth of the body for the building up of itself in love (Ephesians 4:11-16).

These Church offices are commonly called the Five - Fold Ministry Gifts. They are put into place by God to build, unite, equip and encourage Christians. Every fellowship should have these gifts in action.

1. Apostle
2. Prophet
3. Evangelist
4. Pastor
5. Teacher

Group #2 – Manifestation Gifts that REVEAL the POWER of God

There are varieties of effects, but the same God who works all things in all persons. But to each one is given the manifestation of the Spirit for the common good. For to one is given the word of wisdom through the Spirit, and to another the word of knowledge according to the same Spirit; to another faith by the same Spirit, and to another gifts of healing by the one Spirit, and to another the effecting of miracles, and to another prophecy, and to another the distinguishing of spirits, to another various kinds of tongues, and to another the interpretation of tongues. But one and the same Spirit works all these things, distributing to each one individually just as He wills.

For even as the body is one and yet has many members, and all the members of the body, though they are many, are one body, so also is Christ. For by one Spirit we were all baptized into one body, whether Jews or Greeks, whether slaves or free, and we were all made to drink of one Spirit.

For the body is not one member, but many (1 Corinthians 12:6-14).
1. **Word of Wisdom**
2. **Word of Knowledge**
3. **Faith**
4. **Gifts of Healing**
5. **Effecting of Miracles**
6. **Prophecy**
7. **Distinguishing of Spirits**
8. **Kinds of Tongues**
9. **Interpretation of Tongues**

Group #3 – Motivational Gifts REVEAL the NATURE and WAYS of God

Since we have gifts that differ according to the grace given to us, each of us is to exercise them accordingly: if prophecy, according to the proportion of his faith; if service, in his serving; or he who teaches, in his teaching; or he who exhorts, in his exhortation; he who gives, with liberality; he who leads, with diligence; he who shows mercy, with cheerfulness (Romans 12:6-8).

1. Prophecy
2. Service
3. Teaching
4. Exhorting

5. Giving
6. Leading
7. Mercy

Individual Gifts of the Holy Spirit Overview

Group #1 – Church Leadership Offices	Greek Word	Gifts that REVEAL and DIRECT the CORPORATE PLAN of PLAN of God
1. Apostle	*apostolos*	• a delegate, messenger, one sent forth with order
2. Prophet	*proph t s*	• an interpreter of oracles or of other hidden things ; one who, moved by the Spirit of God and hence his organ or spokesman, solemnly declares to men what he has received by inspiration, especially concerning future events, and in particular such as relate to the cause and kingdom of God
3. Evangelist	*euaggelist s*	• a bringer of good tidings
4. Pastor	*poim n*	• a herdsman, especially a shepherd • the presiding officer, manager, director, of any assembly
5. Teacher	*didaskalos*	• to teach • to hold discourse with others in order to instruct them, deliver didactic discourses • to be a teacher
Group #2 – Power Gifts	**Greek Word**	**Manifestation Gifts that REVEAL the POWER**
1. Word of Wisdom	*sophia*	• wisdom, broad and full of intelligence; used of the knowledge of very diverse matters • the wisdom which belongs to men • specifically the varied knowledge of things human and divine, acquired by acuteness and experience, and summed up in maxims and proverbs • the science and learning • the act of interpreting dreams and always giving the sagest advice • the intelligence evinced in discovering the meaning of some mysterious number or vision • skill in the management of affairs • devout and proper prudence in intercourse with men not disciples of Christ, skill and discretion in imparting Christian truth

		• the knowledge and practice of the requisites for godly and upright living • supreme intelligence, such as belongs to God • the wisdom of God as evinced in forming and executing counsels in the formation and government of the world and the scriptures
2. Word of Knowledge	*gn sis*	• knowledge signifies in general intelligence, understanding • specific understanding of a technical nature • the general knowledge of Christian religion • the deeper more perfect and enlarged knowledge of this religion, such as belongs to the more advanced
3. Faith	*pistis*	• conviction of the truth of anything, belief; in the NT of a conviction or belief respecting man's relationship to God and divine things, generally with the included idea of trust and holy fervor born of faith and joined with it • relating to God • the conviction that God exists and is the creator and ruler of all things, the provider and bestower of eternal salvation through Christ • a strong and welcome conviction or belief that Jesus is the Messiah, through whom we obtain eternal salvation in the kingdom of God • belief with the predominate idea of trust (or confidence), springing from faith in God.
4. Gifts of Healing	*iamas*	• a means of healing, remedy, medicine • a healing
5. Effecting of Miracles	*dynamis*	• Strength power, ability • inherent power, power residing in a thing by virtue of its nature, or which a person or thing exerts and puts forth power for performing miracles • moral power and excellence of soul • the power and influence which belong to riches and wealth
6. Prophecy	*proph teia*	• a discourse emanating from divine inspiration and declaring the purposes of God, whether by reproving and admonishing the wicked, or comforting the afflicted, or revealing things hidden; especially by foretelling future events
7. Distinguishing of Spirits	*diakrisis*	• a distinguishing, discerning, judging heart
8. Kinds of Tongues	*gl ssa*	• a tongue • the language or dialect used by a particular people distinct from that of other nations

9. Interpretation of Tongues	herm neia	• interpretation • of what has been spoken in a message of tongues
Group # 3 – **Motivational Gifts**	**Greek Word**	**REVEAL the NATURE and WAYS of God**
1. Giving	metadid mi	• to impart, to share, to provide for a need sacrificially
2. Service	antil mpsis	• to aid, help and give assistance in the work of the ministry
3. Exhorting	parakale	• to call to one's side, call for, summon • to address, speak to, (call to, call upon), which may be done in the way of exhortation, entreaty, comfort, instruction, etc. • to admonish, exhort
4. Teaching	didaskalos	• to hold discourse with others in order to instruct them, deliver didactic discourses • to be a teacher
5. Leading	proïst mi	• to set or place before • to set over • to be over, to superintend, preside over • to be a protector or guardian
6. Mercy	elee	• to have mercy on • to help one afflicted or seeking aid • to help the afflicted, to bring comfort and compassion Motivational Gifts

The Excellence of Love

If I speak with the tongues of men and of angels, but do not have love, I have become a noisy gong or a clanging cymbal. If I have the gift of prophecy, and know all mysteries and all knowledge; and if I have all faith, so as to remove mountains, but do not have love, I am nothing. And if I give all my possessions to feed the poor, and if I surrender my body to be burned, but do not have love, it profits me nothing" (1 Corinthians 13).

You and I should desire to have as many of the gifts of the Spirit in operation in our life as possible. That is just another way of saying that our goal is to act like Jesus. And just like Him, the highest manifestation of God's presence is to love. As Paul wrote in 1 Corinthians 13, everything else really doesn't matter.

THE CHURCH

For the equipping of the saints for the work of service, to the building up of the body of Christ (Ephesians 4:12).

When you hear the word "church" what comes to mind? Do you think of a pretty brick building with a steeple? Or maybe you think of a denomination like Catholic, Baptist or Assembly of God?

The Christian church should be seen in two ways: the visible and the invisible.

1. The visible church is comprised of all who claim the name of Christian and who gather together for worship and participation of the sacraments: the Lord's Supper, Baptism and others. The members of the visible church claim the name of Christian (excluding the cults like the Mormons and Jehovah's Witnesses, etc.). The visible church contains both believers and non-believers; that is, there are people in the visible church who are not really saved.

2. The invisible church is the actual Body of Christ. They are the ones who are truly regenerate and have trusted, by faith, in the Lord and Savior, Jesus Christ. The true Christian is indwelt by the Lord Jesus (John 14:23) through the Holy Spirit. Therefore, the Christian church is figuratively said to be the Body of Christ.

- Rom. 12:5: *So we, who are many, are one body in Christ, and individually members one of another.*
- Eph. *4:12: For the equipping of the saints for the work of service, to the building up of the body of Christ.*

Church Defined
The word "church" comes from the Greek "ekklesia" which means "gathering" or "assembly." Therefore, the church is the gathering of the believers who come together to participate in fellowship with one another as they worship God and hear from His Word, the Bible.

The church as a whole has been equipped with people possessing different spiritual gifts (Rom. 12:5-8). The purpose of the gifts is *for the equipping of the saints for the work of service, to the building up of the body of Christ; until we all attain to the unity of the faith, and of the knowledge of the Son of God, to a mature man, to the measure of the stature which belongs to the fullness of Christ* (Eph. 4:12-13).

Church History
The Christian church was founded by Jesus; He is its Head and Savior (Col. 1:18; Eph. 5:23). It was birthed at Pentecost with the Baptism of the Holy Spirit.

Church Organization
Being in the church, a Christian is subject to the Lordship of Jesus (Eph. 5:24) through the administration of the Word of God.

The Bible does not provide a detailed method of Church government. But, it does state that there are to be elders who govern in the church. These elders are appointed by the laying on of hands (1 Tim. 4:14; 2 Tim. 1:6). They are to be able to teach sound doctrine and refute error (Titus 1:9; 1 Tim. 3:2).

The purpose of the church is to glorify God, fellowship with

Him, and inform and demonstrate to the world the work, love and call of Christ as Redeemer.

Bible description of the Church in action:
They were continually devoting themselves to the apostles' teaching and to fellowship, to the breaking of bread and to prayer. Everyone kept feeling a sense of awe; and many wonders and signs were taking place through the apostles. And all those who had believed were together and had all things in common; and they began selling their property and possessions and were sharing them with all, as anyone might have need. Day by day continuing with one mind in the temple, and breaking bread from house to house, they were taking their meals together with gladness and sincerity of heart, praising God and having favor with all the people. And the Lord was adding to their number day by day those who were being saved (Act 2: 42-47).

I don't want to step on any toes here, but all Christians who are serious about knowing God and being used by Him should be involved in a local church. As the president of Cornerstone Television Network, I want to tell you that watching anointed Christian programming is very valuable. We have seen millions of people touched by God and their lives changed. But no television or radio station or Internet site or book or magazine takes the place of the local church.

I realize that many people are not able to go to church for a lot of different reasons. If you are one of them, then I encourage you to reach out and become involved with other Christians for prayer and fellowship – even if it is limited to talking on the telephone. One of the devil's attack plans is to isolate and convince us that we are the only ones facing challenges and that God doesn't care. That is a lie! I love what Paul says in I Corinthians 10:13: *No temptation has overtaken you but such as is common to man; and God is faithful, who will not allow you to be tempted beyond what you are able, but with the temptation will provide the way of escape also, so that you will be able to endure it.*

Here is the Don Black paraphrase: You are not alone in the challenges that you are facing. In fact, they are pretty common. God knows and He will not allow you to be pushed too far. He will give you a back-door-way-of-escape to get through them. Keep watching for it.

For most of us, it's simple to find a church and start attending. If, however, you need to find a place of worship, we are happy to refer you to a church in your area. Call to find out more. Here is my outline on how you can be an active part of the spiritual dynamic of the local church and not just a spectator. If you do these things, you will share an eternal part in the ministry.

1. How to prepare to be the Church:
   a. Before the service
     i. Pray for wisdom, understanding and knowledge for the following:
       1. Leadership
       2. Members
       3. Visitors
       4. Community
   b. Confession – Make sure your heart is pure and your hands are clean; confess and repent of any sin of which you are convicted.
   c. Expectation – Imagine something great is going to happen in the service. Think of receiving and giving a blessing to someone.

2. Worship – Start at home and in the car.
   a. Put on your favorite worship music.
   b. Tell your family and friends what you are expecting to happen; make a list.

   c. During the service engage in worship. Forget about those around you.

3. Prayer – Be aggressive in seeking God.
   a. Activate Intercessory Prayer
      i. Platform Ministry Team
      ii. Technology Team
      iii. Equipment
   b. Engage in Praise and Worship.
   c. Thanksgiving

4. Express and Grow in Love with God.
   a. Trust in God.
   b. Teaching – Come to learn the truth.
      i. Bring your Bible.
      ii. Take Notes.
   c. Stewardship
      i. Tithes
      ii. Offerings
   d. Personal Spiritual Gifts
      i. Be sensitive to the Spirit's leading.
   e. Discernment
      i. Know what is going on around you.
   f. Ministry time prayer. Don't watch; engage in prayer. Use your Heavenly prayer language.

5. After Service
   a. Linger and watch for opportunities.
   b. Meet new people.
   c. Share.

HEALTHY
RELATIONSHIPS

Whatever you do in word or deed, do all in the name of the Lord Jesus, giving thanks through Him to God the Father. Wives, be subject to your husbands, as is fitting in the Lord. Husbands, love your wives and do not be embittered against them. Children, be obedient to your parents in all things, for this is well-pleasing to the Lord. Whatever you do, do your work heartily, as for the Lord rather than for men (Colossians 3:17-20, 23).

As Christians, every aspect of our life should be dedicated to giving the Lord honor and glory, even through times of trial. Right now, perhaps you are reeling from a revelation of infidelity, considering divorce, dealing with the loss of a loved one, praying fervently for the salvation of unsaved family members, or suffering some other attack against your marriage and family. Whatever your struggle, remember that God has the strength and power to rescue, refine, renew, and restore.

RESCUE
Though the Word never promises a trouble-free, easy life for those who follow Christ, we are guaranteed that the Lord will never leave us nor forsake us (Deuteronomy 31: 6). We are to expect persecution when we are following God's will and doing His work effectively; the devil would not need to attack anyone outside of God's will! In whatever trial you're facing with your marriage or family, remember that this time is temporary—there is a brighter morning ahead. As God promises in Isaiah 51:11, *So the ransomed of the Lord will return and come with joyful shouting to Zion, and everlasting joy will be on their heads. They will obtain gladness and joy, and sorrow and sighing will flee away.*

REFINE

God is using this situation to further mold you to His will: *But we all, with unveiled face, beholding as in a mirror the glory of the Lord, are being transformed into the same image from glory to glory, just as from the Lord, the Spirit* (2 Corinthians 3:18). This present struggle does not change the fact: *And we know that God causes all things to work together for good to those who love God, to those who are called according to His purpose* (Romans 8:28).

RENEW

When you face trials with your loved ones, it's easy to give in to the feelings of defeat and exhaustion. But the Lord has so much better in store for you! He desires you to walk in victory, even when the path is uncertain. Isaiah 40:31 promises, *Yet those who wait for the Lord will gain new strength; They will mount up with wings like eagles, they will run and not get tired, they will walk and not become weary.* Draw closer to God, stay in His Word, and continue in community with your church and Christian friends. The Lord will sustain you!

RESTORE

God is our Restorer. He will… *make up to you for the years that the swarming locust has eaten* (Joel 2:25). God's deepest desire is for you and your family members to live vibrant, abundant Christ-centered lives, with healthy marriages and relationships that serve as a model of Christ's love for His Church. Follow Him and see miraculous healing in your relationships.

More Questions:
How do I survive the loss of a loved one?

Christ has provided all that we need to live a godly life, including the strength to surrender your loved one to God's care and survive the loss and overcome grief with strength and grace. Remember, *But we do not want you to be uninformed, brethren, about those who are asleep, so that you will not grieve as do the rest who have no hope. For if we believe that Jesus died and rose again, even so God will bring with Him those who have fallen asleep in Jesus. For this we say to you by the word of the Lord, that we who are alive and remain until the coming of the Lord, will not precede those who have fallen asleep* (1 Thessalonians 4:13-15). We have a glorious hope of reunion and purpose in life and death though Christ.

How can I have faith for a loved one's salvation?
Do not lose sight of the awesome power of your God, and do not lose faith that He can deliver your loved ones. When Moses doubted God's ability to provide for the children of Israel in the wilderness, the Lord rebuked him, *Is the Lord's power limited? Now you shall see whether my word will come true for you or not* (Numbers 11:23). God's power to save is unlimited. Trust in Him for the salvation of those you love! Center yourself on loving and praying for that person, rather than preaching or nagging them into church attendance. Pray for God to open a door for you to speak the truth in love to them. Most of all, remember your main focus: *You shall love the Lord your God with all your heart, and with all your soul, and with all your strength, and with all your mind; and your neighbor as yourself* (Luke 10:27).

Remember that we are praying for you and your loved ones. God is faithful; He has not forgotten about you! The Lord has told us that when we, His children, agree together on something, He hears and answers our prayers! The day of peace is at hand.

OUR PRAYER FOR YOU TODAY:
Heavenly Father, You say in Your Word that we are not meant to be alone, but need community. Thank You for the people in our lives; loved ones make life together so much sweeter. Pour out Your Spirit on our marriages, children, relatives and friends. Bless our relationships with forgiveness, love, peace and unity. Thank You for Your amazing blessing of salvation! For those we love who don't know You, we know You have not forgotten them. Bring them into Your kingdom, Father, and grant us opportunities to speak truth into their lives. Your will be done. In Jesus' Name, Amen.

FAITH FOR A
GOOD MARRIAGE

It is not good that the man should be alone; I will make him a helper as his partner (Genesis 2:18).

The Bible's instructions for a healthy marriage and family go like this:

> *Do everything in the name of the Lord Jesus, giving thanks to God the Father through him. Wives, be subject to your husbands, as is fitting in the Lord. Husbands, love your wives and never treat them harshly. Children, obey your parents in everything, for this is your acceptable duty in the Lord* (Colossians 3:17-20, 23).

Because everything in a Christian's life should be done in the name of the Lord and for His glory, our marriages and families should glorify God. We at Cornerstone Television believe that you can have faith to overcome the devil's attacks on your marriage and family.

At this moment, you may be reeling from a revelation of infidelity, considering a divorce, just staying together for the children, or suffering some other attack against your marriage. Whatever struggle you may be going through, remember that God has the strength and power to rescue, revive, renew and restore.

Can a Christian marriage be troubled?

Some Christians believe that if they are in God's will, life will be a pleasure cruise. This magical thinking leads them to believe that if they are giving the right amount of money to the church, spending the right amount of time in prayer and Bible study, doing enough witnessing, that there will never be adversity in their lives—and certainly no marriage trouble or divorce!

But that doctrine is not to be found in the Bible. In fact, the Bible tells believers to expect persecution. The devil would not bother to attack anyone outside God's will. But when a Christian spouse or couple is actually doing the Lord's work effectively—that's when the devil jumps in to try to stop them!

And while you wait on the Lord's deliverance, here are some things to keep in mind:

- God still loves you! No matter how bleak things may look, the words of the Apostle Paul are still true for you. *For I am convinced that neither death, nor life, nor angels, nor rulers, nor things present, not things to come, nor powers, nor height, nor depth, nor anything else in all creation, will be able to separate us from the love of God in Christ Jesus our Lord* (Romans 8:38-39).

- God is using this situation to mold you to His will. This present struggle does not change the fact that *...all things work together for good for those who love God, who are called according to His purpose* (Romans 8:28).

- As you draw closer to God, He will comfort and sustain you. Stay in His Word; keep close to your Christian friends and church; and concentrate on prayer, praise, and worship. God is with you and will prevail! *What then are we to say about these things? If God is for us, who is against us? He who did not withhold His own Son, but gave Him up for all of us, will He not with him also give us everything else?* (Romans 8:31-32).

- God's design is for man and wife to be unified, according to Genesis 2:24: *Therefore a man leaves his father and mother and clings to his wife, and they become one flesh.* This isn't just a reference to sexual union, but of the intimacy of life and spirit which God intends for husband and wife to share.

Even in a marriage of committed Christians, the concept and practice of forgiveness is crucial to the maintenance of that intimacy and harmony in the home. If you have been hurt by a spouse's actions, pray and study God's Word on forgiveness and learn to forgive. If you have wounded your spouse through careless actions, seek forgiveness from your mate and from God.

If the strain on the relationship is too heavy, you may want to consult with your pastor or a trained Christian counselor. It is not admission of weakness to seek the help of an expert—and when such help is available, it is wasteful not to reach out for it. (Even if your spouse refuses marriage counseling, you may find much value in conferring with your pastor or Christian counselor alone.)

If you are considering divorce, definitely seek the help of a trained Christian counselor, and bear in mind that the only grounds for divorce given in the Bible are adultery and unwillingness of a non-Christian spouse to stay with a Christian—and of course, you cannot stay with or expose your children to a physically abusive spouse.

But God's deepest desire is to see you and your mate living vibrant Christian lives with a healthy marriage that serves as a model of Christ's love for His church.

You can live that life and see healing in your marriage as you keep Jesus at the center of your thoughts and actions.

God's promise when you feel overwhelmed by the struggle:

Isaiah 51:11 is God's promise that although you may be experiencing trouble in your marriage and family right now, there is a brighter morning ahead of you: *So the ransomed of the Lord shall return and come to Zion with singing; everlasting joy shall be upon their heads; they shall obtain joy and gladness, and sorrow, and sighing shall flee away.*

Remember that we are praying with you for the restoration of your marriage.

THIS IS OUR PRAYER FOR YOU TODAY:

Heavenly Father, Your Word advises husbands to love their wives as much as You loved us and gave Your life for us. You command that wives should serve their husbands with the same love with which they serve You. Pour out your Spirit now on the marriage of Your precious child, and bless this union with forgiveness, love and harmony. In Jesus' Name, Amen.

The Lord has told us that when we, His children, agree together on something, He hears and answers our prayers!

FAITH FOR YOUR LOVED ONE'S SALVATION

The Lord is not slow about his promise...but is patient with you, not wanting any to perish but all to come to repentance (2 Peter 3:9).

Jesus Christ, the only begotten Son of God, came to this earth on a divine rescue mission and gave His life so that sinners like you and me could be born again to His Kingdom.

At such a cost, God does not want anyone to "waste" this sacrifice by refusing to repent and give his/her life to Jesus.

That's one reason we believe that you can have faith that your loved ones will be born again, and that you will see them in heaven! Just as Jesus went about forgiving sin when He walked this earth, He is still present to forgive and receive our loved ones into His Kingdom today.

Jesus has the Father's love for the lost. He demonstrated it in the parables of Luke 15 when He told of the woman rejoicing over the lost coin she had found, and the father rejoicing over the return of his prodigal son. Christ even compared Himself to the shepherd who had found the lost lamb:
   Rejoice with me, for I have found my sheep that was lost (Luke 15:6).

Your loved one is just as loved by the Lord, and Jesus desires to save that stray sheep.

Is it my fault they're not saved yet?

Because of the importance of soul-winning to God and to the church, some Christians have come to believe that if you have not brought everyone in your home, office, and health club to Jesus, then you are not really doing your job as a Christian.

Is that what Jesus said? When He defined our "job" as Christians, He said, *You shall love the Lord your God with all your heart, and with all your soul, and with all your strength, and with all your mind; and your neighbor as yourself* (Luke 10:27). If these are your daily actions, then you have not failed to follow the Lord's commands.

Yes, the Father wants us to share the Good News of salvation through Jesus with all those who have not heard or accepted His invitation. But the fact that you have friends or family members who have not yet come to Christ does not mean that you are a failure as a Christian.

Even the Apostle Paul felt the pain of caring for someone who didn't follow Christ. He lamented, *Demas, in love with this present world, has deserted me and gone to Thessalonica* (2 Timothy 4:10). Was Paul a failure as a Christian? Of course not.

As he knew, it is heartache to see those you love lost and hopeless in spiritual darkness...but you cannot make them accept Christ as Savior. That work of conviction is the province of the Holy Spirit, and He will bring it about in His timing.

Perhaps nothing hurts as much as seeing someone you love reject the love of Jesus. Not only are they rejecting the loving embrace of Almighty God to shelter and comfort them on this earth, but they are also rejecting eternal salvation, risking separation from you and from God forever.

At Cornerstone Television, we understand that pain and we feel privileged to pray for you on behalf of your lost loved one.

Galatians 6:2 commands, *Bear one another's burdens, and in this way you will fulfill the law of Christ.* We will bear this burden with you.

But take heart! The book of Acts gives examples of the faith of individuals being rewarded with salvation of their entire household. In Acts 16:31, the jailer asked Paul and Silas how he could be saved, and they told him, *Believe on the Lord Jesus, and you will be saved, you and your household.*

Likewise, the household of Lydia came to Christ because of her faith (Acts 16:14-15), and in Acts 10 and 11, we read of Cornelius who was visited by an angel and told, *Send to Joppa and bring Simon, who is called Peter; he will give you a message by which you and your entire household will be saved* (Acts 11:13-14). When Peter came, the Holy Spirit fell on Cornelius and the family and friends he had gathered to hear the message!

Never doubt that the faith of one can bring an entire family into the Kingdom of God. In fact, the Old Testament modeled this theme for us when the blood of a lamb had to be shed for atonement: Each family's sins could be covered with one sacrificial lamb—small families could even share the sacrifice. How much more powerful and far-reaching is the power of the sacrifice of the Lamb of God!

> *If, because of one man's trespass, death exercised dominion through that one, much more surely will those who receive the abundance of grace and the free gift of righteousness exercise dominion in life through the one man, Jesus Christ. Therefore just as one man's trespass led to condemnation for all, so one man's act of righteousness leads to justification and life for all* (Romans 5:17-18).

Jesus' sacrifice was intended to bring "life to all," and that includes your lost loved ones. And because God has such a desire to see your friends and family members saved, you can have strong faith that it will happen, no matter what the circumstances are! Your loved one may have no interest in God, may profess to be an atheist, an agnostic, a Hindu—and yet the Holy Spirit will not be deterred.

As you wait and pray for that day of salvation, there are also some things you can do to show your lost loved one—and all those in your sphere of influence—the way to Jesus.

• Live a victorious Christian life. As you concentrate on your own walk with the Lord, you provide a godly example. Even if some of them do not obey the Word, they may be won over without a word by their wives' conduct, when they see the purity and reverence of their lives (I Peter 3:1-2).

• Pray earnestly. James 5:16 says, *The prayer of the righteous is powerful and effective.*

• Speak the truth as God opens the door. Preaching or nagging at your loved ones will do more harm than good, but when the Holy Spirit gives you a natural opening, provide a loving witness. *In your hearts sanctify Christ as Lord. Always be ready to make your defense to anyone who demands from you an accounting for the hope that is in you; yet do it with gentleness and reverence* (1 Peter 3: 15, 16).

This is your duty to the lost, and it can guide them to the Savior, no matter what obstacles may seem to be in the way. Do not lose sight of the awesome power of your God, and do not lose faith that He can deliver your loved ones. When Moses doubted God's ability to provide for the children of Israel in the wilderness, The Lord rebuked him. *Is the LORD's power limited? Now you shall see whether my word will come true for you or not* (Numbers 11:23).

God's power to save is unlimited. Trust in Him for the salvation of those you love!

You may not even be able to imagine the moment when that loved one of yours lets down the defense and allows the Holy Spirit to work. But God has promised in His Word that nothing is impossible with Him! *Ah Lord GOD! It is you who made the heavens and the earth by your great power and by your outstretched arm! Nothing is too hard for you. You show significant love to the thousandth generation* (Jeremiah 32: 17:18).

No matter how far your friend or family member may be from God today, there is nothing so difficult that God cannot accomplish it—especially when His people are united in faith and prayer.

THIS IS OUR PRAYER FOR YOUR LOST LOVED ONE TODAY:

Heavenly Father, You have abundantly blessed us with the free gift of salvation, and for this we are so grateful! Now let our lost brother or sister accept this free gift of God and be born again into Your kingdom. In Jesus' Name, Amen.

The Lord has told us that when we, His children, agree together on something, He hears and answers our prayers! The day of salvation is at hand.

SURVIVING THE LOSS
OF A LOVED ONE

This hope we have as an anchor of the soul, a hope both sure and steadfast and one which enters within the veil (Hebrews 6:19).

Right now, it may seem that your grief is so strong that you cannot even imagine a day when you won't feel sad, lost, and hopeless without your loved one.

But the Bible tells us, *With people this is impossible, but with God all things are possible* (Matthew 19:26).

You can have faith to overcome the pain of loss and live a victorious Christian life in spite of your grief. If it is true that "time heals all wounds," then it is certainly true that time spent with God will also heal and comfort you.

Second Peter 1:3 says of Jesus, *Seeing that His divine power has granted to us everything pertaining to life and godliness, through the true knowledge of Him who called us by His own glory and excellence.*

Christ has provided all that we need to live a godly life, including the strength to surrender your loved one to God's care and survive the loss with strength and grace. As we pray together for your victory, we believe that God will show Himself strong on your behalf.

Do Christians grieve?

Some Christians give party-type funerals for their loved ones, and the atmosphere is so festive that you wouldn't know anyone had died—there's praise and worship, funny stories, affirmation that... *to live is Christ, and to die is gain* (Philippians 1:21).

That's a beautiful way for believers to memorialize our Christian family members who go home to be with the Lord. But maybe you don't feel like celebrating.

Maybe you feel downcast that your loved one will no longer be here to support you, care about you or talk and laugh with you. Maybe you feel lonely and sad without your dear one beside you.

Does that mean you lack faith? Does your grief displease God?

Absolutely not!

In 2 Samuel, when David received the news that his best friend Jonathan had been killed along with King Saul, he did not have a celebration. He cried like a baby.

> *Then David took hold of his clothes and tore them, and so also did all the men who were with him. They mourned and wept and fasted until evening for Saul and his son Jonathan and for the people of the LORD and the house of Israel, because they had fallen by the sword* (2 Samuel 1:11-12).

You can give vent to your emotions and know that God hears your cries and understands your pain. He also lost a loved one to cruel death.

How then can we live? (Ezekiel 33:10).

Sometimes it feels as if we cannot go on living without the strength and company of our loved one who has died. But the fact is, as long as we rely on Jesus day by day, we can continue to live in victory.

And the Bible gives us good examples for how to express our grief and then let it go so that we can "live again" after the death of one dear to us.

In fact, the example of David's behavior in 2 Samuel, after the loss of his best friend Jonathan, can be of great help to us. After he wept and mourned, David then turned his thoughts to the good things he remembered about his friend and the many accomplishments of Saul and Jonathan. He honored their memory.

> *And he told them to teach the sons of Judah the song of the bow; behold, it is written in the book of Jashar. Your beauty, O Israel, is slain on your high places! How have the mighty fallen!*

> *From the blood of the slain, from the fat of the mighty, the bow of Jonathan did not turn back, and the sword of Saul did not return empty. Saul and Jonathan, beloved and pleasant in their life, And in their death they were not parted; They were swifter than eagles, They were stronger than lions. O daughters of Israel, weep over Saul, who clothed you luxuriously in scarlet, who put ornaments of gold on your apparel* (2 Samuel 1:18-19, 22-24).

When you and your family and friends gather together, don't be afraid to talk about the good things you remember about your lost loved one, and honor that memory as David did. Remember the good.

David also acknowledged the power of death on this earth. We, too, must accept the inevitability of death—denial will only prolong our pain. David's example is sure. He mourned his friends with words of acceptance of their fate:

How have the mighty fallen in the midst of the battle! Jonathan is slain on your high places. I am distressed for you, my brother Jonathan; You have been very pleasant to me. Your love to me was more wonderful than the love of women. How have the mighty fallen, And the weapons of war perished! (2 Samuel 1:25-27).

Death is one of the central realities of life and cannot be denied. Acknowledging it and releasing our loved one to God is the ultimate test of our faith.

There's one further biblical step to grieving—one that you and I as believers must take comfort in. We must realize that for the Christian, death is not the end!

Our grief can be tempered with the knowledge that we will be reunited with our loved ones. The Scripture admonishes:
But we do not want you to be uninformed, brethren, about those who are asleep, so that you will not grieve as do the rest who have no hope. For if we believe that Jesus died and rose again, even so God will bring with Him those who have fallen asleep in Jesus. For this we say to you by the word of the Lord, that we who are alive and remain until the coming of the Lord, will not precede those who have fallen asleep (1 Thessalonians 4:13-15).

Paul writes that he does not want the Thessalonians to grieve like the rest of men, but he does not say they shouldn't grieve. Of course, Christians grieve!

But our grief is not hopeless. *This hope we have as an anchor of the soul, a hope both sure and steadfast and one which enters within the veil, where Jesus has entered as a forerunner for us, having become a high priest forever according to the order of Melchizedek* (Hebrews 6:19-20).

God's promise for overcoming the pain of grief...

Isaiah 51: 11 is God's promise that while you may feel sad and alone today, there is a brighter morning ahead of you:

So the ransomed of the LORD will return and come with joyful shouting to Zion, and everlasting joy will be on their heads. They will obtain gladness and joy, and sorrow and sighing will flee away.

Let the love of God sustain you and focus on His goodness. King David wondered, *Why are you in despair, O my soul? And why are you disturbed within me? Hope in God, for I shall again praise Him, The help of my countenance and my God* (Psalm 43:5).

Although you may feel cast down today, you will emerge from this grief. And remember that we are praying with you for comfort and peace in this time of bereavement.

GOD IS OUR PROVIDER

Our Heavenly Father doesn't play favorites. He loves you and cares about every area of your life – including finances! King David attests to this fact in Psalm 37:25, *I have been young and now I am old, yet I have not seen the righteous forsaken or his descendants begging bread.* God will never forsake you!

As Paul reminds us in Hebrews 13:5, *Make sure that your character is free from the love of money, being content with what you have; for He Himself has said, 'I will never desert you, nor will I ever forsake you'.*

Perhaps you're looking for employment or recently lost your job. Or maybe you're facing a stack of bills or loans to repay and the realization you are barely able to support your family. Financial burdens can seem so hopeless and all consuming. However, God's provision is miraculous! He is our Shepherd who meets all of our needs with perfect timing. Whatever struggle you're going through, God has the strength and power to rescue, refine, renew, and restore you and your finances!

RESCUE
Though the Word never promises a trouble-free, easy life for those who follow Christ, we are guaranteed that the Lord will never leave us nor forsake us (Deuteronomy 31:6). We are to expect persecution when we are following God's will and doing His work effectively. In whatever financial trial you're facing, remember that this time is temporary—there is a brighter morning ahead. As God promises in Isaiah 51:11, *So the ransomed*

of the Lord shall return and come to Zion with signing; everlasting joy shall be upon their heads; they shall obtain joy and gladness, and sorrow and sighing shall flee away.

REFINE

God is using this situation to further mold you to His will: *Consider it all joy, my brethren, when you encounter various trials, knowing that the testing of your faith produces endurance. And let endurance have its perfect result, so that you may be perfect and complete, lacking in nothing* (James1:2-4). This present struggle does not change the fact that *we know that God causes all things to work together for good to those who love God, to those who are called according to His purpose* (Romans 8:28).

RENEW

When you face money trials, it's easy to give in to the feelings of defeat and exhaustion. But the Lord has so much better in store for you! He desires you to walk in victory, even when the path is uncertain. Isaiah 40:31 promises, *Yet those who wait for the Lord will gain new strength; they will mount up with wings like eagles, they will run and not get tired, they will walk and not become weary.* Draw closer to God, stay in His Word, and continue in community with your church and Christian friends. The Lord will sustain you! *When you pass through the waters, I will be with you; and through the rivers, they will not overflow you; when you walk through the fire you will not be scorched nor will the flame burn you* (Isaiah 43:2).

RESTORE

God is our Restorer—He will make up to you for the years that the swarming locust has eaten (Joel 2:25). God's deepest desire is for you to live a vibrant, abundant Christ-centered life, free from the chains of debt and despair. You are a child of the King who owns the *cattle on a thousand hills* (Psalm 50:10)—and He has promised to care for you! The King is your source and supply! Don't become so focused on the financial struggle that you miss out witnessing God's great miracle in your life.

So what should I do next?

- **Tithe:** In order to truly prosper, God must have total control over every area of your life. Commit to honor God with your finances through tithing, which is giving 10% of your income to your church. Although it may seem difficult to do this during times of financial famine, God asks us to test Him on His faithfulness in this area. He promises a blessing to those who tithe: *Bring the whole tithe into the storehouse, so that there may be food in my house, and test me now in this, says the Lord of hosts, if I will not open for you the windows of heaven and pour out for you a blessing until it overflows* (Malachi 3:10).

- **Give to Those in Need:** Tithing is your obligation to God, but what you give to His work and to the poor above your regular 10% is considered sowing a seed. When you plant such a seed of faith, believe that God will bring about a harvest in your life. Jesus often used the analogy of planting and harvest to show us how our good works and charitable giving bring rewards in our own lives.

- **Work to be Debt-Free:** Proverbs 22:7 tells us, *The rich rule over the poor, and the borrower becomes slave of the lender.* As Christians, we are called to live in freedom! Freedom from debt is a major step towards abundant life. Connect to a personal economics workshop like Dave Ramsey's Financial Peace Program! Beginning this process will help you achieve confidence in your finances.

- **Count your Blessings:** Sometimes during trying circumstances, negativity weighs us down. We tend to forget that the JOY of the Lord is our strength (Nehemiah 8:10)! Make a list of everything you have to be thankful for; whether this is a one-time list or a daily log of thankfulness, it will encourage and uplift you! The Apostle Paul advises in Philippians 4:8, *Finally, brethren, whatever is true, whatever is honorable, whatever is right, whatever is pure, whatever is lovely, whatever is of good repute, if there is any excellence and if anything worthy of praise, dwell on these things.* Don't let despair be a stronghold in your life.

Let the love of God sustain you and focus on His goodness. King David wondered, *Why are you in despair, O my soul? And why are you disturbed within me? Hope in God, for I shall again praise Him, the help of my countenance and my God* (Psalm 43:5). Do not be afraid to tell the Lord that your soul is cast down. And remember that we are praying with you.

THIS IS OUR PRAYER FOR YOU TODAY:

Heavenly Father, We are grateful and privileged to call You Father. We are thankful that You have adopted us as Your children. Today we ask for Your miraculous provision in every area of life and a fulfillment of every need. In Jesus' Name, Amen.

MONEY MATTERS

I have been young and now I am old, yet I have not seen the righteous forsaken or his descendants begging bread Psalm 37:25.

King David knew the faithfulness of God and you can, too! God will not forsake you or leave your children to live in poverty.

At Cornerstone Television we believe in God's miraculous provision!

You can have faith to overcome the devil's attacks on your finances. Perhaps you are looking for a job or have just lost your job. Maybe you are facing a stack of bills you can't pay and are barely able to feed your family. Whatever struggle you may be going through, remember that God has the strength and power to rescue, revive, renew and restore.

Second Peter 1:3 says of Jesus, *Seeing that His divine power has granted to us everything pertaining to life and godliness, through the true knowledge of Him who called us by His own glory and excellence.*

Christ has provided all that we need, including the solutions for our financial struggles.

Do real Christians have financial trouble?

In some Christian circles, the leaders teach that when you are in God's will, no tragedy can ever strike you. They believe that somewhere in the Bible it says if you win souls, give to the church, pray and read the Scriptures, then you will never have any obstacles to your success – and certainly no financial troubles!

But that doctrine is false! Look at the tragedies which befell the disciples of Jesus after His ascension: they were imprisoned, beaten, and even killed. No one would say that these martyrs were out of God's will. No one would doubt their Christianity.

The Bible tells believers to expect persecution. So if you are experiencing trouble in your finances, do not take it as a sign that you lack faith in God, are out of God's will or have been rejected by God.

If you have been foolish with your money, then yes, you must change! But if you have been a good manager of the funds which God has entrusted to you and still find yourself in financial straits, then this persecution may be further proof that God is with you. We read in James 1:2-4: *Consider it all joy, my brethren, when you encounter various trials, knowing that the testing of your faith produces endurance. And let endurance have its perfect result, so that you may be perfect and complete, lacking in nothing.*

It's best to keep in mind that what's yours is really God's – in money matters and in every area of life.

So then let no one boast in men. For all things belong to you, whether Paul or Apollos or Cephas or the world or life or death or things present or things to come; all things belong to you, and you belong to Christ; and Christ belongs to God (I Corinthians 3:21-23).

At Cornerstone Television we believe that in order to prosper you, God must have control of every area of your life. God can restore your finances. This is what we are praying for, but it probably won't happen until you have committed to honor God.

The first way to do that with regard to your finances is to tithe. "Tithing" means giving 10% of your income to the Lord. Although it may be difficult to make this sacrifice, Deuteronomy 4:23 commands that the tithe be given to the Lord. In Malachi 3:10, God promises a blessing on those who tithe: *Bring the whole tithe into the storehouse, so that there may be food in My house, and test Me now in this, says the LORD of hosts, if I will not open for you the windows of heaven and pour out for you a blessing until it overflows.*

Cornerstone Television regularly tithes 10% of the money donated; we support Christian ministries worldwide with our tithe. Your tithe belongs to God to be used to do His Kingdom's work.

The next way to honor God in your finances is through following His command to provide for your family. The Apostle Paul said, *But if anyone does not provide for his own, and especially for those of his household, he has denied the faith and is worse than an unbeliever* (I Timothy 5:8).

And the third way to honor God with your finances is to give to those in need, and support the work of missions and evangelism. Paul records the liberality of the poor Macedonian church as they gave to needy Christians elsewhere:
> *That in a great ordeal of affliction their abundance of joy and their deep poverty overflowed in the wealth of their liberality. For I testify that according to their ability, and beyond their ability, they gave of their own accord, begging us with much urging for the favor of participation in the support of the saints* (II Corinthians 8: 2-4).

Tithing reflects your obedience to God, but what you give to His work and to the poor above your regular 10% is considered sowing a seed. When you plant such a seed of faith, believe that

God will bring about a harvest in your life. Jesus often used the analogy of planting and harvest to show us how our good works and charitable giving bring rewards in our own lives. It can be a struggle to manage tithing, giving and providing for your family, but if you put God first in your life, it can be done.

Here are three biblical ideas for wise stewardship which may help you today:

- Understand your stewardship responsibilities. There are many fine books by Christian financial advisors and teachers which will show you how to budget, how to invest, how to save – in general: practical, biblical principles for getting our finances in order. You would be wise to take advantage of this teaching.

- Live as simply as possible. Belt-tightening is never easy, but it can bring huge benefits.

- Remember that GOD IS YOUR SOURCE! Your job is just one channel of God's blessing, and God is the source of supply for you. If you become so focused on your financial struggle that you fail to consider the awesome power of God to rescue and restore, you may miss your miracle!

What then shall we say to these things? If God is for us, who is against us? He who did not spare His own Son, but delivered Him over for us all, how will He not also with Him freely give us all things? (Romans 8:31-32).

You are a child of the King, and God has promised to care for you. Do not be downhearted. Remember that God is your source.

Trust in the Lord for your deliverance!

God's promise when you feel overwhelmed by the struggle...

Here is God's promise that although you may be experiencing trouble in your finances right now, He will not forsake you: *When you pass through the waters, I will be with you; and through the rivers, they will not overflow you. When you walk through the fire, you will not be scorched, nor will the flame burn you* (Isaiah 43:2).

Remember that we are praying with you for the restoration of your finances.

THIS IS OUR PRAYER FOR YOU TODAY:

Heavenly Father, You have abundantly blessed us with the free gift of salvation, and for this we are so grateful! Your Word tells us that we should ask what we will in Your Name, and You will provide it. Today we ask for a financial miracle in the life of Your child. In Jesus' Name, Amen.

The Lord has told us that when we, His children, agree together on something, He hears and answers our prayers!

YOU ARE GOD'S BELOVED

27

GOD'S ANSWER

But as for me, I trust in You, O LORD; I say, 'You are my God. My times are in Your hand; Deliver me from the hand of my enemies and from those who persecute me.' (Psalm 31:14-15).

You are God's child and He loves you!

At Cornerstone Television, we have learned that no matter what circumstances may surround us, when we are surrendered to the will of God, nothing can stop God's purposes for us.

This is true in your life, too!

We believe that even as Jesus ministered to the oppressed when He physically walked the earth, so He still delivers His children from their trials today.

The Apostle Paul reminds us of the depth of God's love for us:
For I am convinced that neither death, nor life, nor angels, nor principalities, nor things present, nor things to come, nor powers, nor height, nor depth, nor any other created thing, will be able to separate us from the love of God, which is in Christ Jesus our Lord (Romans 8:38-39).

Remember as you await God's answer to your prayers, nothing can take you from the loving embrace of your Father.

Our Heavenly Father desires the best for you!

As a child of the King, you are a joint heir with Christ. This is God's view of you, and if you will surrender your life to Him completely, He will see that you receive what is most needful for you—and your family too.

Jesus opens His arms wide to you today and waits to gather you in, saying: *Come to Me, all who are weary and heavy-laden, and I will give you rest. Take My yoke upon you and learn from Me, for I am gentle and humble in heart, and you will find rest for your souls. For My yoke is easy and My burden is light* (Matthew 11:28-30).

If you have never accepted Christ's free gift of forgiveness and asked for your birthright as a child of God, simply do it today.

Understand that sin separates every human from a relationship with God. His perfect Son, Jesus, came to this world to offer Himself as a sacrifice for sin. He accepted the punishment which you and I deserve because of our sin nature. When we confess our sin to Him and ask forgiveness, He cleanses us so that we can be in communion with God and receive the rewards of a child of God.

Let Jesus cleanse you from sin today!

The Bible assures us, *Beloved, now we are God's children* (1 John 3:2), and again: *For you have not received a spirit of slavery leading to fear again, but you have received a spirit of adoption as sons by which we cry out, "Abba! Father!" The Spirit Himself testifies with our spirit that we are children of God, and if children, heirs also, heirs of God and fellow heirs with Christ, if indeed we suffer with Him so that we may also be glorified with Him* (Romans 8:15-17).

Because of your status as God's child, you can receive the power of the Holy Spirit to live in victory, no matter what the physical circumstances.

Jesus said. *These things I have spoken to you, so that in Me you may have peace. In the world you have tribulation, but take courage; I have overcome the world* (John 16:33).

The peace of the Lord is God's gift to you. Even when you have needs in your life and family, you can still feel the peace of God and assurance in your salvation. At Cornerstone Television, we believe that prayer plays a tremendous role in seeing miraculous answers to our deepest needs; so we are privileged to pray with you.

And as you await the answer to your prayers, you can live in victory by understanding and following these steps toward joy and encouragement:

- **Pray.** This is key to close communion with God. You can share all your most heart-felt needs with Him and He will understand. *Cast your burden upon the LORD and He will sustain you; He will never allow the righteous to be shaken* (Psalm 55:22).

- **Worship the Lord.** The Bible says *God is holy, enthroned on the praises of Israel* (Psalm 22:3 ESV). To be sure that the Lord is ever present in your life to strengthen and comfort you, keep Him enthroned on your praises.

- **Study the Word.** *Your word is a lamp to my feet and a light to my path* (Psalm 119:105). Whatever you need, you can find the answer in God's Word.

- **Go to church.** According to 1 Corinthians 12, the body of Christ needs you and you need to be a vital member of this body, too. Fellowship with Christian brothers and sisters will help you in your Christian walk and help to keep you encouraged and joyful.

- **Count your blessings.** Whenever you feel challenged by circumstances, make a list of everything for which you are thankful. It will encourage you! The Apostle Paul advised: *Finally, brethren, whatever is true, whatever is honorable, whatever is right, whatever is pure, whatever is lovely, whatever is of good repute, if there is any excellence and if anything worthy of praise, dwell on these things* (Philippians 4:8).

God loves you and has given His Son Jesus to save you, His Holy Spirit to empower you, His Church to guide and uplift you, and His forgiveness and compassion to comfort and nurture you.

With all this as your birthright, you—as a child of the King—can overcome the trials and temptations of life and feel the joy of the Lord. As you remain committed to God and reliant on His power, you will be secure in the knowledge that others are praying with you. The Lord has declared:
When you pass through the waters, I will be with you; and through the rivers, they will not overflow you. When you walk through the fire, you will not be scorched, nor will the flame burn you (Isaiah 43:2).

Trust in the Lord!

God's promise when you feel overwhelmed…
Isaiah 51:11 is God's promise that while you may face struggle and need in your life today, there is a brighter morning ahead of you:
So the ransomed of the LORD will return and come with joyful shouting to Zion, and everlasting joy will be on their heads. They will obtain gladness and joy, and sorrow and sighing will flee away.

Let the love of God sustain you and focus on His goodness. King David wondered, *Why are you in despair, O my soul? And why are you disturbed within me? Hope in God, for I shall again praise Him,*

The help of my countenance and my God (Psalm 43:5).

Do not be afraid to tell the Lord that your soul is cast down. And remember that we are praying with you.

THIS IS OUR PRAYER FOR YOU TODAY:

Heavenly Father, We are grateful and privileged to call You Father. We are thankful that You have adopted us as Your children. Today we ask for Your miraculous provision in every area of life and a fulfillment of every need. In Jesus' Name, Amen.

The Lord has told us that when we, His children, agree together on something, He hears and answers our prayers! He will meet your needs!

HOW TO PRAY

28

GOD'S ANSWER

Therefore, confess your sins to one another, and pray for one another so that you may be healed. The effective prayer of a righteous man can accomplish much (James 5:16).

And when you are praying, do not use meaningless repetition as the Gentiles do, for they suppose that they will be heard for their many words. So do not be like them; for your Father knows what you need before you ask Him.
Pray, then, in this way:
> *'Our Father who is in heaven,*
> *Hallowed be Your name.*
> *Your kingdom come.*
> *Your will be done,*
> *On earth as it is in heaven.*
> *Give us this day our daily bread.*
> *And forgive us our debts, as we also have*
> *forgiven our debtors.*
> *And do not lead us into temptation, but*
> *deliver us from evil.*
> *For Yours is the kingdom and the power and*
> *the glory forever. Amen.'* (Matthew 6).

We all need a healing, a touch from God! It may be physical, emotional or spiritual. To be healed means to be restored. We need to be put back together in the way God originally assembled us.

I created the following prayer guide to help you pray effectively both for yourself and others. Simply fill in the name in the blank and take it to God. The prayer's wording is not mine but is pulled from Paul's prayers in scripture.

Prayer Part 1 – **Honor God**

Lord, may _____ be filled with the knowledge of Your will in all spiritual wisdom and understanding, so that he/she will walk in a manner worthy of You, to please You in all respects, bearing fruit in every good work and increasing in the knowledge of You.

Father count _____ worthy of Your calling, and fulfill every desire for goodness and the work of faith with Your power.

Prayer Part 2 – **New Hope**

Father, You are the God of hope. Fill _____ with all joy and peace in believing, so that _____ will abound in hope.

Give _____ a spirit of wisdom and of revelation in the knowledge of You. I pray that the eyes of _____'s heart may be enlightened, so that _____ will know what is the hope of Your calling, what are the riches of the glory of Your inheritance in the saints, and what is the surpassing greatness of Your power toward us who believe.

Prayer Part 3 – **Love**

Strengthen _____ with power through the Holy Spirit in the inner man, so that Christ may dwell in _____'s heart through faith; and that _____, being rooted and grounded in love, may be able to comprehend with all the saints what is the breadth and length and height and depth, and to know the love of Christ which surpasses knowledge.

Lord cause _____ to increase and abound in love for all people; so that You may establish _____'s heart without blame in holiness.

That _____'s love may abound still more and more in real knowledge and all discernment, so that _____ may approve the things that are excellent, in order to be sincere and blameless.

Lord direct _____'s heart into your love and into the steadfastness of Christ.

Prayer Part 4 – Power

Strengthen _____ with all power, according to Your glorious might, for the attaining of all steadfastness and patience; joyously giving thanks to You, Who has qualified us to share in the inheritance of His saints in Light.

Father, comfort and strengthen _____'s heart in every good work and word.

You are the God of peace; sanctify _____ entirely, and may _____'s spirit, soul and body be preserved complete.

Father, I lift up _____ . Thank you for answering this prayer. I ask in the name of Jesus. Amen.

Prayer Guide's Scripture References:

Romans 15:13—*Now may the God of hope fill you with all joy and* peace in believing, so that you will abound in hope by the power of the Holy Spirit.

Ephesians 1:16-19—*I do not cease giving thanks for you, while making mention of you in my prayers; [17]that the God of our Lord Jesus Christ, the Father of glory, may give to you a spirit of wisdom and of revelation in the knowledge of Him. [18]I pray that the eyes of your heart may be enlightened, so that you will know what is the hope of His calling, what are the riches of the glory of His inheritance in the saints, [19]and what is the surpassing greatness of His power toward us who believe. These are in accordance with the working of the strength of His might ...*

Ephesians 3:14-19—*For this reason I bow my knees before the Father, [15]from whom every family in heaven and on earth derives its name, [16]that He would grant you, according to the riches of His glory, to be strengthened with power through His Spirit in the inner man, [17]so that Christ may dwell in your hearts through faith; and that you, being rooted and grounded in love, [18]may be able to comprehend with all the saints what is the breadth and length and height and depth, and to know the love of Christ which surpasses knowledge, that you may be filled up to all the fullness of God.*

Philippians 1:9-11—*And this I pray, that your love may abound still more and more in real knowledge and all discernment, [10]so that you may approve the things that are excellent, in order to be sincere and blameless until the day of Christ; [11]having been filled with the fruit of righteousness which comes through Jesus Christ, to the glory and praise of God.*

Colossians 1:9-12—*For this reason also, since the day we heard of it, we have not ceased to pray for you and to ask that you may be filled with the knowledge of His will in all spiritual wisdom and understanding, [10]so that you will walk in a manner worthy of the Lord, to please Him in all respects, bearing fruit in every good work and* *increasing in the knowledge of God; [11]strengthened with all power, according to His glorious might, for the attaining of all steadfastness and patience; joyously [12]giving thanks to the Father, who has qualified us to share in the inheritance of the saints in Light.*

1 Thessalonians 3:12-13—*and may the Lord cause you to increase and abound in love for one another, and for all people, just as we also do for you; [13]so that He may establish your hearts without blame in holiness before our God and Father at the coming of our Lord Jesus with all His saints.*

1 Thessalonians 5:23—*Now may the God of peace Himself sanctify you entirely; and may your spirit and soul and body be preserved complete, without blame at the coming of our Lord Jesus Christ.*

2 Thessalonians 1:11-12—*To this end also we pray for you always, that our God will count you worthy of your calling, and fulfill every desire for goodness and the work of faith with power, [12]so that the name of our Lord Jesus will be glorified in you, and you in Him, according to the grace of our God and the Lord Jesus Christ.*

2 Thessalonians 2:16-17—*Now may our Lord Jesus Christ Himself and God our Father, who has loved us and given us eternal comfort and good hope by grace, [17]comfort and strengthen your hearts in every good work and word.*

2 Thessalonians 3:5—*May the Lord direct your hearts into the love of God and into the steadfastness of Christ.*

WHAT IS FASTING?

Yet even now, declares the LORD, return to Me with all your heart, and with fasting, weeping and mourning... (Joel 2:12).

The purpose of a fast is to establish a point of self-denial of the flesh in order to redirect your mind, body and spirit to God. The Bible provides us examples of both corporate and personal fasting.

Corporate Fasting

Nehemiah 9:1
[The People Confess Their Sin] *Now on the twenty-fourth day of this month the sons of Israel assembled with fasting, in sackcloth and with dirt upon them.*

Esther 4:3
In each and every province where the command and decree of the king came, there was great mourning among the Jews, with fasting, weeping and wailing; and many lay on sackcloth and ashes.

Personal Fasting

Daniel 9:3
So I gave my attention to the Lord God to seek Him by prayer and supplications, with fasting, sackcloth and ashes.

Joel 2:12
Yet even now, declares the LORD, Return to Me with all your heart, And with fasting, weeping and mourning...

Jesus fasted 40 days in the wilderness to prepare for spiritual battle.

Jesus taught on fasting.

Matthew 6:16
Whenever you fast, do not put on a gloomy face as the hypocrites do, for they neglect their appearance so that they will be noticed by men when they are fasting. Truly I say to you, they have their reward in full.

Fasting builds faith.

Matthew 17:21
Then the disciples came to Jesus privately and said, 'Why could we not drive it out?' And He said to them, "Because of the littleness of your faith; for truly I say to you, if you have faith the size of a mustard seed, you will say to this mountain, 'Move from here to there, and it will move; and nothing will be impossible to you.' ["But this kind does not go out except by prayer and fasting."]

Fasting is optional

Scripture does not command Christians to fast. God does not require or demand it. At the same time, the Bible presents fasting as something that is good, profitable, and beneficial. The book of Acts records believers fasting before they made important decisions.

Acts 13:2
While they were worshiping the Lord and fasting, the Holy Spirit said, 'Set apart for me Barnabas and Saul for the work to which I have called them.'

Acts 14:23
And when they had appointed elders for them in every church, with prayer and fasting they committed them to the Lord in whom they had believed.

Fasting is not dieting.

Too often, the focus of fasting is on the lack of food. Instead, the purpose of fasting should be to take your eyes off the flesh and to focus completely on God. Fasting is a way to demonstrate to God, and to ourselves, that we are serious about our relationship with Him. Fasting helps us gain a new perspective and a renewed reliance upon God. Although fasting in Scripture is almost always a fasting from food, there are other ways to fast. Anything given up temporarily in order to focus all our attention on God can be considered a fast (1 Corinthians 7:1-5).

Fasting changes us.

By taking our focus off the things of the flesh, we can more successfully turn our attention to the Spirit. Fasting is not a way to get God to do what we want. Fasting changes us, not God. It is not a way to appear more spiritual than others. Fasting is to be done in a spirit of humility and a joyful attitude.

"Fasting is important, more important, perhaps, than many of us have supposed," said Arthur Wallis in God's Chosen Fast. " ... When exercised with a pure heart and a right motive, fasting may provide us with a key to unlock doors where other keys have failed; a window opening up new horizons in the unseen world; a spiritual weapon of God's providing, 'mighty, to the pulling down of strongholds.'"

Fasting is a tool we can use to fight in our spiritual warfare. Ask God to show you how to incorporate it into your Christian life.

Father, teach me more about prayer and fasting. Holy Spirit, I ask You to open my eyes to Your truth and give me the power to overcome the flesh and walk in victory. I will do anything You desire of me. I love You. I ask this in the name of Jesus. Amen.

THINGS TO COME

We are living in a very exciting time. God is preparing His Church to welcome Jesus back to this world. He is coming this time not as a baby but as a warrior, the King of kings. I believe that we are living in the Kingdom Generation. Great things are just ahead. Time is unveiling a mystery.

God is in total control. He always has been. Lucifer didn't take Him by surprise with his rebellion. It is impossible for you and me to disappoint Him. Why, you ask? Because He knew what we were going to do before we did it. So He has never been disappointed. Take a minute right now and let that truth sink in. It will free you from the ton of condemnation that the devil has you carrying. You may have blown a divine opportunity because of sin and that will cost, but God's Kingdom is intact. In fact, He rules everything seen and unseen.

Our Heavenly Father is getting ready to end this spiritual age. He is preparing for the Rapture of His Church and the Seven Year Tribulation period. Nothing in Heaven or on earth will stand in His way, or delay His plan by a millisecond.

My goal is to help you think differently about life in light of God's Word and the times we live in.

Please understand that I am not trying to judge you, the quality of your life, or your commitment to God. I hope you love Him with all your heart and have a growing relationship with Jesus Christ.

I know He loves you and has a specific plan and purpose for you.

Life moves fast.

We often get so caught up in the details of everyday living and can be distracted from the ones we love and the real spiritual truth of life. We are tempted to take our focus off the "big picture" and look only to the demands of the right-here-right-now.

Thankfully, our Heavenly Father doesn't work that way. He has a laser focus on getting His will done, not just for us individually but also for His Church as a body. Nothing takes Him by surprise, nor can anything change or stop His Kingdom's progress. In fact, in the very real spiritual fourth dimension, it is already finished; Jesus did that at the cross. It is just a matter of waiting a little longer for His physical Kingdom to come, and God has even created this wait time because of His lovingkindness.

In order for His plan to play out, there must first be a great revival in the Church. The Spirit of God is building His Church for the return of Christ. In fact, Jesus predicted that the ...gates of Hell will not prevail against His Church.

Now here is the really great news. Our generation will have the privilege of actually seeing this happen! Friend, it would be very valuable for you to understand what your part in the mystery is. Please be alert to the "signs of the times." Be a good manager of your time, talent and treasures. We are blessed to be witnesses to the end of the age.

It doesn't matter how young or how old you are. Your race and gender aren't important. You have a job to do. The fact that you are alive proves that it is God's plan for you to share in this end day's work. Your place in eternity depends on how you walk in obedience to Him now. As Jesus would often say, "He who has ears let him hear."

CPSIA information can be obtained at www.ICGtesting.com
Printed in the USA
BVOW07s0615131113

336171BV00001B/1/P